THE

VITAL STATISTICS

OF

SHEFFIELD.

BY G. CALVERT HOLLAND, ESQ., M.D.

PHYSICIAN EXTRAORDINARY TO THE SHEFFIELD GENERAL INFIRMARY;
FORMERLY PRESIDENT OF THE HUNTERIAN AND ROYAL
PHYSICAL SOCIETIES, EDINBURGH; AND BACHELOR
OF LETTERS OF THE UNIVERSITY OF PARIS.

LONDON:

ROBERT TYAS, 8, PATERNOSTER ROW;

J. H. GREAVES, SHEFFIELD.

1843.

THE VITAL

STATISTICS OF SHEFFIELD.

TO THOMAS ASLINE WARD, Esq.,

THE TOWN REGENT,

AND TO

THE TOWN TRUSTEES OF SHEFFIELD.

GENTLEMEN,

To no public body can the following pages be inscribed so appropriately as to you. The inquiry was undertaken at your suggestion, and the expenses incurred in the prosecution of it, are in part defrayed by your liberality. The funds which you have at command, arising from an incorporated Trust, which has existed for centuries, are laid out with judgment and economy in local improvements—in charitable purposes, and in the encourage-. ment of undertakings, having an especial relation to the interests of the Town. With several of you, some of the happiest and the most instructive moments of my life have been passed in the confidential intimacies of friendship. Receive my best wishes for your individual welfare, and believe me, truly yours,

G. CALVERT HOLLAND.

Sheffield, July, 1843.

CONTENTS.

INTRODUCTION.

The attention of the writer had been directed for several years to the examination of the social and physical condition of the working classes in this district, and in some branches of the investigation, considerable progress had been made, when he was requested by the Town Trustees to undertake, what was previously not contemplated in his plan, an inquiry into various other circumstances of local interest or importance. The task was cheerfully entered upon, and the results of several years' investigation are embodied in the following pages.

Persons who are not familiar with the labour of statistical researches, can form no conception of the difficulties and embarrassing circumstances which are constantly liable to arrest or retard the progress of them. Ignorance and

B

prejudice are among the most formidable of these difficulties, and, at times, no arguments or representations could
overcome them. It was imagined by the parties interro-
gated, that some deep government scheme lay concealed
beneath the questions proposed.

There is one feature in these statistics which will be
regarded by some as an objection, the writer having presumed to reason on the data presented, as well as to express
an opinion on subjects of delicacy and importance. He
pleads guilty to the charge. The objection does not,
however, in any degree affect the accuracy of the facts
adduced; and those who like not the train of reasoning
pursued, or the opinions expressed, must pardon their
introduction. The object has been, not only to arrive at
important truths, but to interest the mind of the reader in
such researches, indifferent whether he adopt or reject the
views brought under consideration. To awaken his feelings
is to make him an enquirer into facts. A dry detail of
particulars, without comments, would present few attractions
to a mind directed to these studies for the first time. The
table of contents at the end of a book, would possess equal
interest.

The answers, to the inquiries respecting the condition of
the several branches of manufacture examined, throw considerable light on the circumstances of each, as regards the

division of labour—the intelligence—habits and remuneration of the workmen. It must, however, be kept in mind, that the scale of wages, fluctuates with the demand for labour in all branches, except some which are in union. The long continued depression has destroyed the combinations of several since the completion of this inquiry, and the artisans are exceedingly distressed. We shall not dwell on the evils, which we conceive to arise from such changes, as respects the manufacturer—the artisan and the town at large. The delicacy of the subject forbids it, and this is not the place to enter upon the consideration of it. The object of the work is to state facts, and not to record opinions.

There is one part of these statistics which is of great practical value, and may be studied with advantage by certain bodies of individuals, in every manufacturing town, —the writer alludes to the numerous experiments stated, respecting the cheapest and most efficient mode of repairing streets and roads on which the traffic is considerable. None will dispute the value of such experiments. They exhibit, on the part of the intelligent surveyor,* an amount of thought, labour, and analytical power, rarely possessed by persons in such situations. To him the author begs especially to express his obligations, and also, to Mr. Geo. Crossland,

* Mr. William Lee.

the Superintendant Registrar; to Mr. Thomas Raynor, the Police Surveyor; to Mr. Benjamin Spurr; to Mr. John Hardy, and to Mr. John Heppenstall, Upperthorpe, for the services which they have rendered him in these inquiries. Had the difficulties, arising from prejudices opposed to such investigations, been less, numerous additional facts, bearing on the condition of the working classes, would have been brought under notice.

The writer presents his imperfect labours to the public, in the hope that they will incite others to complete what is here only rudely sketched.

CHAPTER I.

GENERAL DESCRIPTION OF THE TOWN AND NEIGHBOURHOOD OF SHEFFIELD.

A few remarks descriptive of the town, and the immediate neighbourhood, to which the following statistical researches relate, will not be altogether void of interest to the reader who is unacquainted with both. There is perhaps no town of the same importance in the kingdom, commanding an equal variety of scenery; soft and sylvan —bold and abrupt—beautiful in all the exquisite touches of a cabinet picture—or presenting to the eye, in extensive or remote prospects, all the comprehensive lineaments of a magnificent panorama.

The *Rivelin* and the *Loxley*, from the West, after supplying numerous *dams* and grinding wheels, and skirting along wooded hills and naked precipices, fall into the Don, a little to the North of the town.

The *Don*, after these additions, runs in a South-Eastwardly direction to the lowest part of the town, where,

being joined by the Sheaf, (from which the town derives
its name,) it turns nearly due North, and flows in the fine
open valley which stretches to Rotherham.

The *Sheaf* enters the precincts of the town, on the
South side, from the picturesque scenery of Abbey Dale and
Beauchief Wood, and takes a course nearly Northward, with
occasional wanderings, previous to being lost in the Don.
About half a mile before it arrives at the point where it
becomes tributary, it receives the waters of the Porter.
This little stream is a native of the parish, springing in
Upper Hallam; and its course is marked by the formation
of tiny lakes,—reservoirs of water,—whence several mills,
forges, and grinding wheels derive their propulsive power;
and these objects give to the valley through which it flows,
an air of enchantment that has long warmed the imagination and enriched the portfolios of artists.

The Don, the Sheaf, and the Porter form three sides
of a peninsulated area, upon which stands the greater part
of the town. The apex of this area is the confluence of
the Sheaf and the Don; on each side of it, but more gently
towards the Sheaf and the Porter than in the direction of
the Don, the apex rises into a boldly swelling hill, the
ridge of which passes through the centre, and the Western
portions of the town, and beyond even its remotest suburbs.
From the confluence of the Sheaf and the Porter rises a
similarly beautiful hill. On the North side of the Don,
the scenery is perhaps still more imposing; the steep
declivity is clothed by forest trees of the Old Park Wood,
over which appears a portion of the pleasant village of
Pitsmoor. The summits and sides of all these hills are,
in the vicinity of the town, studded with neat and elegant

villas—the residences of the gentry and the leading manufacturers and merchants. On the Eastern side of the Sheaf, near its junction with the Don, the Park, covered with dwellings, rises like an amphitheatre above the rest of the town, to a ridge not inaptly termed *Sky Edge*, from which point, under favourable circumstances, almost the whole of Sheffield, and its surrounding villages for a considerable distance, may be discerned.

Elliott has described, in graphic and glowing language, these tributary streams, and the exquisite scenery which they embellish, and from which they borrow much of their own beauty.

> Five rivers, like the fingers of a hand,
> Flung from black mountains, mingle, and are one
> Where sweetest vallies quit the wild and grand,
> And eldest forests, o'er the silvan Don,
> Bid their immortal brother journey on,
> A stately pilgrim, watch'd by all the hills.
> Say, shall we wander, where, through warriors' graves,
> The infant Yewden, mountain-cradled, trills
> Her doric notes? Or, where the Locksley raves
> Of broil and battle, and the rocks and caves
> Dream yet of ancient days? Or, where the sky
> Darkens o'er Rivelin, the clear and cold,
> That throws his blue length, like a snake, from high?
> Or, where deep azure brightens into gold
> O'er Sheaf, that mourns in Eden? Or, where, roll'd
> On tawny sands, through regions passion-wild,
> And groves of love, in jealous beauty dark,
> Complains the Porter, Nature's thwarted child,
> Born in the waste, like headlong Wiming? Hark!
> The pois'd hawk calls thee, Village Patriarch!
> He calls thee to his mountains! Up, away!
> Up, up, to Stanedge! higher still ascend,
> Till kindred rivers, from the summit gray,
> To distant seas their course in beauty bend,
> And, like the lives of human millions, blend
> Disparted waves in one immensity!
>
> VILLAGE PATRIARCH, Page 61.

The delightful localities of the town might, however, have remained a sterile wilderness, or have risen only to the importance of a village, had they not been peculiarly favoured by the possession of vast mineral riches.

The GEOLOGICAL position of Sheffield is the foundation upon which its wealth and commercial enterprise are based.

Iron ore is obtained in large quantities in the immediate neighbourhood. The carboniferous Limestone of Derbyshire, which is used as a flux in smelting, and for other important purposes, is within the distance of a few miles, and the chief cost is that of conveyance. Excellent Coal is also plentiful and cheap; one of the main seams lies indeed under a large portion of the town. The Magnesian Limestone, extensively used for building purposes, can be brought from Conisbro' and other places by water, and sold for a few shillings per ton; while, in every direction, and contiguous to the town, may be found quarries of Freestone of various descriptions, furnishing grinding and millstones, common roofing slate, or flag stones of excellent quality.

With such local advantages, it is not at all extraordinary, that the town should have become celebrated, in every part of the civilized globe, for its cutlery and hardware; and at no period in its history, was it ever more justly distinguished than at present. The skill and genius of its artisans, and the liberality of its enterprising manufacturers, have given a high character to its productions.

The following remarks, descriptive of the immediate scenery of the town, are from the pen of a native,* whose elegance, accuracy, and deep research, give a peculiar value to his observations :—

" The distance of the parish of Sheffield from the Eastern " and Western Seas is nearly equal; and although it is " further from the most Northern point of Scotland than " from the Southern coast of England, yet a line which " might be drawn nearly straight from Liverpool to Hull, " passing through Sheffield, would divide the island into " two nearly equal portions. It lies on the Eastern side " of that high and mountainous tract which Dodworth, who " rarely hazards such a remark, says may be called the " English Appenines ; ' because the rain water which there " falleth sheddeth from sea to sea.' The ridge of this " tract lies nearly in the direction from North to South. " The mountains of Westmoreland, Craven, and the Peak " belong to it, and it is finally lost to the South in the " moorlands of Staffordshire. Sheffield lies rather at the " foot of these hills than among them.

" Qua se subducere colles
" Incipiunt, mollique jugum demittere clivo
" Usque ad aquam."

" The town stands at least at the point of union of many " streams, that become not inconsiderable, which have " their rise amongst those hills, and where the hills are fast " subsiding into that fine level champaigne country which " extends to Doncaster and beyond it."

* The Rev. Joseph Hunter, F.R.S.

" It is in a country like this that we look for the *beautiful*
" in landscape. The grander and more august features
" of nature are to be sought in regions decidedly moun-
" tainous ; and are contemplated with more complete
" satisfaction, where the artificial creations of man have
" not intruded to break the harmony of the scene. But
" the softer graces of landscape are chiefly to be found in a
" district uneven, but not mountainous, and may be con-
" templated with not less pleasure because among them are
" to be found some of the works of human hands. Close
" and well-wooded valleys, with streams glittering along
" them, and the bare scar occasionally peeping through the
" foliage : hills appearing from behind other hills of nearly
" equal altitude, some bearing fine masses of wood, and
" others studded with cheerful villas : views of wonderful
" extent, embracing variety of objects, some of which are
" associated with events of historical importance : these are
" what the vicinity of Sheffield presents to the lovers of
" picturesque beauty, and which never fail to arrest the
" attention of the passing traveller."

The population differs in several important respects from
that of many other manufacturing districts. The labouring
classes are higher in intelligence, morality and physical
condition, than where machinery is extensively used, as
in Manchester, Leeds, Nottingham and Stockport. The
middle classes are a greater proportion of the population
than in these towns. The merchants and manufacturers
among us are not men of large capital, exercising immense
influence. They are very far from treading on the heels
of the aristocracy. These striking differences may be
traced to the degree in which machinery is employed in
the several important branches of manufacture. In this

town, no improvements can supersede, to any great extent, the necessity for adult manual labour, as in the cotton, the woollen, and the silk departments; consequently we perceive less misery, destitution and ignorance among the artisans, and also less of the other extreme—opulence and its extravagances—than in situations where the machine cheapens to the starving point, the labour of the industrious mechanic. Many facts will be adduced in the subsequent pages, in confirmation of these assertions.

Sheffield has also been peculiarly fortunate in possessing, for a series of years, several men of distinguished genius— men indeed who have exercised a vast and beneficial influence on the views, feelings and interests of its inhabitants. The names of James Montgomery,* Ebenezer Elliott,† and Samuel Bailey,‡ are beginning to be felt as household words, not only in the vicinity of their own domestic hearth, but wherever taste and imagination, genius and philosophy are cultivated. One, by the graces of an elegant, chaste and sportive fancy, has awakened pure and elevated thoughts in inseparable association with religion. Another, stern and vigorous in his powers— the unsophisticated child of nature—wayward in passion— but in his touches of what is simple, lovely or magnificent, is without a living equal. His thoughts rush impetuous into concentrated and vivid expression. Lastly, the philosopher

* The author of the " West Indies" and the " World before the Flood," &c.

† Author of the "Village Patriarch," " Love," the " Ranter" and " Corn-Law Rhymes," &c.

‡ Author of the works " On the Formation and Publication of Opinions," " Essays on Truth, Knowledge, Evidence, and Expectation," " A Review of Berkeley's Theory of Vision," &c.

of comprehensive views and high-toned morality, looks beyond the exigencies and expedients of the moment. His page is the embodiment of refined taste—vigorous reasoning—independent thought and searching investigation. The town has great reason to be proud of such men—they will stand out in bold relief in the pages of its history.

The beneficial influence of genius is not to be measured by political or religious distinctions, with which it may be associated. It is a power pregnant with thought, and insinuates itself in endless forms and fashions into the minds of others, stimulating the understanding—awakening its faculties—giving to the external world new attractions, and opening a wider theatre for intellectual exertion. Men who create thought, and, by their labours diffuse around them the charities and the liberalizing influences of humanity, have a value which society never justly estimates. Their worth is too frequently judged by that which is the least in importance, and the most perishable of their reputation—opinions which connect them with existing parties. The comprehensive mind, while it is not insensible of what is good, in the exertions of diversified religious sections and political classified orders, nor averse to co-operate in the attempt to carry out whatever is calculated to promote the interests of man, looks, however, far beyond the narrow views on which such distinctions rest. It is this portion of the mind that belongs to the world at large—to all ages, and to humanity in every stage of progression or change. We honour the presence of genius in all its forms, believing the manifestations of it to be fraught with incalculable benefits, being indeed peculiar laws, impressed upon the minds of the few, to exalt, instruct, delight, or purify, the grosser intellects of mankind.

The man who, by mechanical improvements, facilitates the production of the necessaries of civilized life, is a blessing to his race; and not less so is he who, by the touch of genius, heightens and embellishes the enjoyments of them. The two will ever go hand in hand : the circumstances which suggest and give play to the exertions of the one, are equally favourable to the achievements of the other.

The partiality of a native cannot, however, conceal some other truths, less gratifying to expatiate upon, than the residence amongst us of men of genius. The town has little to boast in the cultivation of science, or in the encouragement given to the fine arts : we fear that to exhibit a taste for either, rather deteriorates than improves the position of an individual in the estimation of the public. The acquisition of wealth is accompanied with little solicitude to exalt the intellectual character. The town has a philosophical and literary institution—museum, and a society for the study and encouragement of works of art; but these do not receive that liberal support which they deserve. It may justly boast of possessing a Botanical Garden surpassed by none in the kingdom, in the taste of its arrangements and the beauty of its situation, and yet, with these advantages, it is lamentably neglected by the public.

The noblemen who have important interests in the town are, his Grace the Duke of Norfolk and the Earl Fitzwilliam. The former possesses a very valuable property in it; and while the town has to acknowledge numerous munificent donations from his Grace and a long line of distinguished ancestry, it would be unjust to pass over in silence, the taste, judgment and enterprise of his agent*—qualities exhibited in local improvements and suggestions, to the advantage of the social and physical condition of the population, and redounding equally to that of his noble employer. The last act of this illustrious family, and which is now being carried into effect, is laying out an extensive plot of ground for the recreation and sports of the working classes. This consideration reflects infinite credit on the benefactor.

The town is also under great obligations to two noblemen, resident in the immediate neighbourhood—the Right Hon. the Earl Fitzwilliam, and the Right Honourable the Lord Wharncliffe. The services of both have been a series of liberal and enlightened acts.

Among the many improvements which have taken place in this town, within the past few years, none have been more beneficial than the ample supply of water, conveyed in pipes through all the principal streets, and accessible to the inhabitants three days in the week. A deficiency is rarely felt in the driest summers.

The total surface area of the reservoirs of the Water Company is about 63 acres, containing, when full, nearly 45 millions of cubic feet of water.

The principal store Reservoir, is situate at Redmires, about seven miles West of the town, and at an elevation of about eleven hundred feet above the level of the sea. The water covers an area of about forty-eight acres, and in some places is upwards of forty feet deep.

* Michael Ellison, Esq.

The supply is derived from the surface drainage, or gather of upwards of a thousand acres of land, in its immediate vicinity; that is to say, from the rain descending upon that surface, and it will naturally be imagined that the quantity will be very abundant at such an elevation above the sea.* The rain guage, in one year, indicated a depth of forty-nine inches.

The Company is, however, restricted by Act of Parliament, from taking any water into the reservoir until the mills below, on the river Rivelin are satisfied, which point is ascertained by means of a weir, placed at Redmires for that purpose.

The water is conveyed from Redmires into the Service Reservoir at Crookes, at a distance of one mile from the town, by means of an open conduit, lined with stone, and thence is distributed throughout the town by cast iron pipes of various calibre, from eighteen to three inches in diameter, into which the leaden branches of the tenants are inserted.

Crookes Reservoir is situate at an elevation of four hundred and sixty feet above the lower parts of the town, so that any inhabitant may be accommodated with water at the top of his house, and without extra charge, as is the case in London, and other places where propulsive power is required to effect this.

* The rain-clouds, generally tending Eastward, are intercepted by the range of hills, extending North and South, through the centre of the Northern Counties; and this accounts for a greater fall of water at or near this elevation, contrary to the usual fact that most rain falls in the lowest situations.

The Company supply nearly every house in the town most abundantly. They are prepared with the present means to meet a much greater demand than can exist for years. The water is, necessarily, from its source, of the purest quality.

The charges or rents are amongst the lowest, if not the very lowest in the kingdom, especially for the poorer classes of houses, being fifty per cent. lower than at Manchester and Birmingham, London and Newcastle.

Besides houses, the company supply many steam engines, breweries and manufactories of various kinds.

There are nearly forty miles of cast iron pipes in the town, and some few miles of old wooden pipes, for which iron pipes are rapidly being substituted, so that in the course of a year or two, all vestige of the old system will be extinct.

The neighbourhood of Sheffield is not particularly distinguished by the variety of its vegetable productions. Though the surface of the country presents considerable diversity in regard to aspect and elevation, the prevailing character of the soil is that of yellow loamy clays, with a variable admixture of sand. On the Moors, to the North and South-West of the town, the soil is formed of earthy and mineral constituents, commonly designated sandy-peat, of which extensive tracts exist, exceedingly bleak and barren, with comparatively little bog. Numerous local changes, accompanied by the rapid decrease of wood in the vicinity of the town, have materially lessened the attractions and treasures of well known and frequently explored districts. Any one deeply interested in the subject will perceive to what extent the botanical riches have disappeared, by examining the valuable and well preserved dried specimens of our late honoured townsman Mr. Salt, as well as his manuscript collectanea towards a Flora of the neighbourhood, both of which are now the property of the Philosophical Society of Sheffield. Many species are described by him that will in vain be sought in the places which, some years ago, were their common habitats. The botanist, however, will still find many plants that will well repay the labour of the search. To facilitate his inquiries, the subjoined particulars are given respecting the rarer plants, and the sites in which they are found.

On the wet and boggy parts of the Moors, about five miles from the town, the following species, among many others, are found :—

Andromeda polifolia.
Drosera rotundifolia.
Drosera longifolia.
Drosera Anglica.
Epilobium palustre.
Epilobium tetragonum.
Eleocharis palustris.
Eleocharis cœspitosa.
Eriophorum vaginatum.
Eriophorum angustifolium.
Eriophorum polystachyon.
Juncus uliginosus.
Juncus uliginosus var. B. vivi parus.
Listera cordata.
Narthecium ossifragum.
Pinguicula vulgaris.
Rynchospora alba.
Vaccinium Vitis-Idœa
Vaccinium Oxycoccos.

On the dryer and more elevated parts, the following may be met with :—

Aira præcox.
Arctostaphylos Uva ursi.
Cerastium semidecandrum.
Epilobium montanum.
Erica tetralix, and a variety having white flowers.
Empetrum nigrum.
Juncus squarrosus.
Nardus stricta.
Rubus idæus.
Ulex nanus.
Ulex nanus var. B. major.

c

In the woods and fields nearer the town :—

Achillæa Ptarmica.
Alchimilla arvensis.
Alchimilla vulgaris.
Alchimilla vulgaris var. B. minor.
Alisma Plantago.
Allium ursinum.
Alopecurus agrestis.
Alsine rubra.
Alsine tenuifolia.
Anagallis arvensis.
Arenaria serpyllifolia.
Arundo Epigejos.
Atriplex laciniata.
Barbarea præcox.
Barbarea stricta, new to Britain and recorded in the recently published fifth edition of Sir W. J. Hooker's British Flora, as growing along the railroads near Sheffield.
Bartsia odontites.
Brachypodium sylvaticum.
Bromus asper.
Bromus erectus.
Bromus squarrosus.
Callitrichie verna.
Cardamine amara.
Carex ovalis.
Carex remota.
Carex pendula.
Carex sylvatica.
Carex præcox.
Carex binervis.
Carex recurva.
Catabrosa aquatica.
Cerastium tetandrum.
Cerasus avium.
Cerasus padus.
Chenopodium glaucum.
Chrysoplenum alternifolium.
Cichorum Intybus.
Circæa Lutetiana.

Dianthus deltoides.
Elymus europæus.
Epipactis catifolia.
Euphorbia helioscopica.
Euphorbia exigua.
Festuca gigantea.
Fumaria capreolata.
Galium saxatile.
Geranium columbinum.
Gnaphalium dioicum.
Hordeum pratense.
Hypericum quadrangulum.
Hypericum pulchrum.
Lamium galeobdalon.
Lathræa squamaria.
Lepidium campestre.
Lithospermum arvense.
Lycopsis arvensis.
Lycopus europœus.
Lysimachia nummularia.
Melampyrum pratense.
Melampyrum sylvaticum.
Melilotus officinalis
Millium effusum.
Mœhringia trinervis.
Myosotis collina.
Myosotis versicolor.
Nasturtium terrestre.
Nepeta cataria.
Ornithopus perpusillus.
Orobus tuberosus.
Orobus tuberosus var. B tenuifolius
Papaver argemone
Papaver dubium.
Phalaris arundinacea.
Prunus institia.
Ribes alpinum.
Rosa arvensis.
Sanicula europæa.
Saponaria officinalis.
Sarothamnus scoparius.
Saxifraga granulata.

Scabiosa succisa, variety with white flowers.
Sclerochloa rigida.
Scrophularia nodosa.
Senecio viscosus.
Senecio erucæfolius.
Serratula tinctoria.
Sisymbrium Thalianum.
Stellaria nemorum.
Stellaria uliginosa.
Teesdalia nudicaulis.
Trifolium medium.
Trifolium arvense.

Trisetum flavescens.
Valeriana dioica.
Vicia angustifolia.
Vicia tetrasperma.
Vicia tetrasperma var. B.gracili s.
Viola palustris.
Viola odorata. This universal favourite, which is rare in this locality is seldom found with blue flowers; we have the white variety, which is not inferior in its agreeable scent.
Viola arvensis.

Of the exceedingly beautiful and interesting tribe of Ferns, and allied Genera, the neighbourhood affords great variety. The following are the different species, whether common or otherwise, growing wild, which the writer has met with.

Asplenium Adiantum-nigrum.
Asplenium Ruta-muraria.
Asplenium Trichomanes.
Athyrium Filio Fæmina var. B. irrigium.
Botrychium Lunaria.
Ceterach Officinarum. This plant, a few years ago, grew in considerable plenty on Heely bridge; by the ravages of thoughtless collectors it has however, been destroyed.
Cistopteris fragilis.
Lastræa Filix-mas.
Lastræa Oreopteris.
Lastræa dilatata.
Lomaria spicant.
Ophyoglossum vulgatum.
Osmunda regalis.

Polypodium Dryopteris.
Polypodium Phegopteris.
Polypodium vulgare.
Polystichum aculeatum.
Polystichum lobatum.
Pteris Aquilina.
Pteris Aquilina, var. contracta (mihi.)
Scolopendrium vulgare.
Scolopendrium vulgare, var. multifidum.
Equisetum arvense.
Equisetum limosum.
Equisetum limosum, var. nudum.
Equisetum palustre.
Equisetum sylvaticum.
Lycopodium alpinum.
Lycopodium clavatum.
Lycopodium Selago.

In the lower Cryptogamic tribes, such as Mosses, Lichens &c., this locality is particularly rich.

c 2

The wood-crowned hills surrounding Sheffield, once abounded in objects of interest to the Ornithologist; but the destructive axe, and the more destructive strolling grinder, have caused the rarer birds to disappear, whilst those formerly common are now equally scarce. The Buzzard (Buteo fuscus) is no longer to be seen soaring over the Old Park wood. Kingfishers, (Alcedo Ispida,) Sandpipers, (Tringa hypoleucos,) and Little Grebes, (Podiceps minor,) may still occasionally be found along the rivers and brooks. Notwithstanding the progress of the axe, numerous birds are still found in the neighbourhood of this populous town. The following have come under our immediate inspection :—

Rough legged Buzzard (Buteo lagopus)—Eight or ten have been seen and procured.

Osprey (Pandion Haliaëtus)—Three have been obtained, in the course of ten years; one at Hillsbro' fish pond, another, in 1838, on the edge of Bradfield moor, and a very fine specimen at Whirlow.

Brown-bee Hawk (Pernis apivora)—Wharncliffe wood has furnished three specimens, Tinsley park one, and Ecclesall wood one of this rare Hawk. Few localities can boast of such a number.

Peregrine Falcon (Falco Peregrinus)—Three of these birds have been shot lately: two are in the collection of M. J. Ellison, Esq. We observed one fly over the Infirmary in the spring of 1840. This is the species famed in falconry.

The Hobby (F. Subbuteo)—Merlin (F. Æsalon)—are seen every year. Kestrels (F. Tinnunculus) are pretty plentiful.

Marsh Harrier (Circus Cyaneus)—occasionally seen; one shot on Hallam moors.

Owls are scarce here. The following are sometimes found :— Hooting Owl, (Ulula Aluco,) Long and Short Eared Owls, (Asio Otus and A. brachyotus.)

Night-jar (Caprimulgus Europeus)—The Moors.

Grey Fly-catcher (Muscicapa grisola)—Common.

Pied Fly-catcher (M. atricapilla)—The park Wharncliffe; sometimes in the vicinity of the town.

Bombycilla garrula (Waxwing)—Many of these beautiful birds have at various times visited our locality.

Red backed Shrike (Lanius Collurio)—Used to be found about Steel bank, but is now almost extinct. A few sometimes are in the valley of Loxley.

Long billed Chough (Fregilus Graculus)—One was shot on the Subscription Moors.

Grey Wagtail (Motacilla Boarula)—Breeds on the Moors—is found about the town in the winter—acquires its summer plumage before it retires. A few M. Yarelli stay the winter over.

Dipper (Cinclus Europeus)—This lively little bird is not unfrequent along the Moor streams; it is quite a local species.

Ring Thrush (Turdus torquatus)—Plentiful on the Moors—visits the gardens near the town, feeding on currants, cherries, &c.

Philomela Luscinia (Nightingale)—Is sometimes in the Old Park wood—said to have been heard in Ecclesall wood, but perhaps the rich notes of Sylvia hortensis or atricapilla have been mislaken for this charming songster.

The following Titmice are common:—Parus fringillago, cæruleus ater palustris, and longicaudata. In their company are Regulus aurocapillus and Certhia familiaris.

The Green Woodpecker (Picus viridis and Picus pipra are occasionally found. A male and female of Picus Striolatus were shot in Middlewood.

The Wry-neck (Yunx torquilla)—Once frequented the Rivelin, but now is scarcely ever seen.

Snow Bunting (Plectrophanes nivalis)—visits the moors every year—one obtained in a garden adjoining Pitsmoor Workhouse.

Mountain Finch (Fringilla montifringilla)—Not uncommon in the winter season.

Coccothraustes atrogularis (Grosbeak)—Has been shot near Heely, but not recently.

The Lesser Redpole (Linaria minor)—Breeds abundantly. Linaria borealis (Mealey Redpole)—One shot in the Infirmary gardens.

Carduelis Spinus (Siskin)—Not unfrequent.

Common Crossbill (Loxia Europea)—Has been seen in many fir plantations about the town.

The Stock dove (Columba Œnas)—Is often intermingled with small flocks of Ring Doves (C. Palumbus) in Wharncliffe and other woods.

Columba Turtur (Turtle Dove)—One was shot near the Blast Furnace; others have been obtained a few miles from the town.

The game birds of the locality are Phasianus Colchicus, (Pheasant,) Perdix Cinerea. (Partridge)—(the Quail is said to have been heard near Brightside)—Tetrao Tetrix, (Black Grouse,) on some moors; Lagopus Scoticus, (Red Grouse,) plentiful where preserved.

Herons (Ardea major)—Frequently fly over the town, but seldom find a fishing place sufficiently secluded.

Bittern—Little London dam and Ecclesall wood.

Numenius Phæopus (Whimbrel—On the Moors is not unfrequently obtained.

Woodcocks, Snipes and Judcocks are not uncommon; the former sometimes breed in the neighbourhood.

Charadrius pluvialis (Golden Plover)—Rather frequent.

C. Morinellus (Dotterell)—Sometimes on the Moors.

Ring Plover—Shot near the reservoir at Redmires.

Crested Grebe (Podiceps Cristatus)—One or two have been caught in an exhausted state.

Sterna Hirundo, (Common Tern,) Sterna Minuta, (Little T. and S. Fissipes Black T—Shot on Blonk dam and various parts of the river.

Larus Argentatus, Canus and Tridactylus, (Herring, Common and Kittiwake gulls)—Often fly over, and a good many are shot, mostly young birds.

Stormy Petrel (Procellaria pelagica)—One is said to have been shot on a house in Waingate, by Mr. Raven, watchmaker.

Anser ferus (Grey lag Goose)—Frequently fly over; sometimes settle in the wheat fields.

Mallards (Anas boschas) and Teal (Anas crecca)—Are obtained most winters.

Anas Clangula (Golden eye Duck)—Fine specimens have been shot on Little London dam and at Brightside lane.

One hundred and thirty species have been obtained in the neighbourhood. Of these, fifty-one are resident, forty are stragglers, and thirty-nine are migratory.

Quadrupeds found in the neighbourhood of Sheffield. Those marked * are very rare.

*Badger,	Meles Taxus.
*Marten,	Mustela Foina.
Pole-cat,	M. putorius.
Weasel,	M. vulgaris.
Stoat,	M. erminea.
*Otter,	Lutra vulgaris.
Fox,	Vulpes vulgaris.
Mole,	Talpa Europea.
Common Shrew,	Sorex Utragonurus.
Water Shrew,	Sorex fodiens.
Hedge hog,	Erinaceus Europeus.
Pipistrelle.	Vespertilio Pipistrellus.
Greater long eared bat,	Vespertilio Auritus.
Squirrel,	Sciurus vulgaris.
Dormouse,	Myoxus avellanarius.
Field Mouse,	Mus sylvaticus.
House Mouse,	Mus musculus.
Rat,	Mus decumanus.
Water Rat,	Arvicola Amphibia.
Hare,	Lepus Timidus.
Rabbit,	Lepus Cuniculus.

The following Fishes may be found in the Don, and other streams of our locality.

Perch,	Perca fluviatilis.
Ruffe,	Perca Cernua.
Bull-head,	Cottus gobio.
Carp,	Cyprinus Carpio.
Barbel,	Cyprinus Barbus.
Gudgeon,	Cyprinus gobio.
Tench,	Cyprinus tinca.
Bream,	Cyprinus brama.
Roach,	Cyprinus rutilus.
Dace,	Cyprinus Leuciscus.
Chub,	Cyprinus Cephalus.
Bleak,	Cyprinus Alburnus.
Minnow,	Cyprinus Phoxinus.
Loach,	Cobitis barbatula.

Pike,	Esox lucius.
*Salmon,	Salmo salar.
Trout,	Salmo Fario.
Grayling,	Thymallus vulgaris.
Eel,	Anguilla acutirostris.
River Lamprey,	Petromyzon fluviatilis.

The temperature, atmospheric pressure and the fall of rain, observed for two years in succession.

1837.		
RAIN	BAROMETER.† MONTHLY MEAN.	THERMOMETER.* MONTHLY MEAN.
Jan...... 3,92 Inchs.	Jan......... 29,35 Ins.	Jan. ...... 36,1 Dgrs.
Feb. ... 2,93 ...	Feb. .... 29,23 ...	Feb. ...... 39,1 ...
March.. 2,58 ...	March .... 29,36 ...	March ... 35,5 ...
April... 2,36 ...	April ...... 29,18 ...	April...... 44,6 ...
May ... 1,59 ...	May ...... 29,29 ...	May ...... 50,1 ...
June ... 1,88 ...	June ...... 29,37 ...	June...... 60,0 ...
July ... 2,45 ...	July ...... 29,04 ...	July ...... 65,7 ...
Aug. ... 2,52 ...	Aug. ...... 29,33 ...	Aug. ...... 60,3 ...
Sept. ... 1,60 ...	Sept. ...... 29,06 ...	Sept. ...... 55,3 ...
Oct. ... 2,77 ...	Oct......... 29,22 ...	Oct. ...... 49,9 ...
Nov. ... 2,02 ...	Nov. .... 28,90 ...	Nov. .... 41,0 ...
Dec. ... 3,10 ...	Dec. ...... 29,05 ...	Dec. ...... 40,2 ...
Total, 29,72 Inches	Annual M. 29,18	Annual M. 48,1 Ins.
1838.		
Jan. ... 2,08 ...	Jan. ...... 29,27 ...	Jan. ...... 27,1 Dgrs.
Feb. ... 4,01 ...	Feb. ...... 28,88 ...	Feb. ...... 28,5 ...
March.. 2,75 ...	March ... 29,07 ...	March ... 43,0 ...
April... 2,00 ...	April...... 29,02 ...	April...... 42,8 ...
May ... 3,48 ...	May ...... 29,37 ...	May ...... 50,5 ...
June ... 3,46 ...	June ...... 29,21 ...	June...... 59,0 ...
July ... 3,30 ...	July ...... 29,25 ...	July ...... 60,2 ...
Aug. ... 2,27 ...	Aug. ...... 28,90 ...	Aug. ...... 60,5 ...
Sept. ... 1,93 ...	Sept. ...... 29,19 ...	Sept. ...... 56,0 ...
Oct. ... 4,45 ...	Oct. ...... 29,12 ...	Oct. ...... 45,0 ...
Nov. ... 2,01 ...	Nov. .... 28,83 ...	Nov. .... 38,0 ...
Dec. ... 0,80 ...	Dec. ...... 29,20 ...	Dec. ...... 40,0 ...
Total. 32,54 Inches	Annual M. 29,11 Ins.	Annual M. 45,9 ...

* Very rare now, but formerly was sometimes caught at Brightside weir.

† Three observations daily.

1837.—Rainy days, 176—Overcast, 115—Fine, 35—Hard frost, 22—Hoar frost, 16—Clear sunshine, 1.

1838.—Rainy days, 173—Overcast, 48—Fine, 54—Hard frost, 21—Hoar frost, 6—Clear sunshine 0—Days depositing snow, sleet of hail, 63.

NOTE.—The above observations were taken at the Intake, an elevation of 470 feet above the level of the river Don. The Thermometer was constantly in the open air in the shade, exposed to the North, so as to be as little affected as possible by the sun's rays

CHAPTER II.

THE RATE OF INCREASE IN THE POPULATION.

There are few manufacturing towns that have advanced more rapidly in wealth and population than Sheffield. The subjoined statements show the immense increase in the latter within the period of one century. The increased wealth cannot be measured. Were this possible, it would be found in a much greater ratio than that of population. The numerous villas which adorn the neighbouring hills— the expensive establishments—the costly equipages—the manifest command of luxuries and comforts unknown to the same class of manufacturers, forty years ago, indicate an amount of progress, perfectly startling to the sober calculations of men, strangers to the productive powers of commerce.

The wealth of the town cannot, however, be compared with that of many other places, such as Manchester, Leeds, or even Birmingham; nor does the trade carried on admit of the creation of splendid fortunes. Many of the branches are efficiently conducted with a small capital—a few hundred pounds,—requiring neither extensive premises, costly or complicated machinery; hence the prevalence of small masters, and the competition necessarily resulting, prevent the aggregation of masses of wealth.

It is stated, on good authority, that at the middle of the past century, there was only one house of sufficient enterprise or importance in the town, to send a traveller abroad, and now persons of this character are employed in every part of the civilized world.

POPULATION OF THE SEVERAL TOWNSHIPS, COMPRISING THE PARISH OF SHEFFIELD, FROM THE YEAR 1736.

TOWNSHIPS.	POPULATION.						
	1736.	1801.	1811.	1821.	1831.	1840.	1841.
Sheffield	9,095	31,314	35,840	42,157	59,011	73,856	69,587
Brightside Bierlow....	983	4,030	4,899	6,615	8,968	11,772	10,089
Ecclesall Bierlow....		5,362	6,569	9,113	14,279	20,263	19,984
Hallam (Nether)......	2,352	1,974	2,384	3,200	4,568	6,296	7,275
Hallam (Upper)......		797	866	1,018	1,035	1,121	1,401
Attercliffe-cum-Darnall..	1,076	2,281	2,673	3,172	3,741	4,352	4,156
TOTAL....	14,105	45,758	53,231	66,275	91,692	117,662	112,492

The population of 1840 was an estimate formed on the known rates of increase in preceding periods, aided, also, by occasional inquiries instituted by the authorities of the town, in connexion with proposed municipal changes. Reasoning on these data, the population was imagined to have increased in nine years, from 91,692 to 117,660, but which the Census of 1841 shews to be an exaggeration. The estimate, however, is retained, as reference will be made to it in subsequent remarks

POPULATION RETURNS FOR 1881.

TOWNSHIPS.	Sheffield.	Ecclesall.	Brightside.	N.Hallm.	U.Hallm.	Attercliff.	Total.
Number of inhabited Houses.	12,144	2,519	1,790	905	189	783	18,331
Number of Families.	12,609	3,579	1,853	964	189	804	19,998
Houses Building	266	165	9	26	1	1	468
Uninhabited Houses.	652	186	41	53	7	25	914
Families employed in Agriculture	66	214	26	52	54	31	443
Families employed in Trade, Manufactures and Handicraft.	9,849	2,659	1,843	725	89	429	14,734
Not in either of these Classes.	3,054	706	484	187	46	344	4,821
Males	29,483	7,078	4,356	2,319	535	1,874	45,465
Females	29,528	7,201	4,612	2,339	500	1,867	46,047
Total	59,011	14,279	8,968	4,658	1,035	3,741	91,692
Males twenty years old	15,455	3,397	1,860	1,107	266	958	23,043
Occupiers of land, employing Labourers.	5	38	10	12	16	23	104
Occupiers of land, not employing Labourers.	34	22	19	12	37	4	128
Labourers employed in Agriculture.	78	187	44	51	54	4	418
Males employed in manufactures, or making manufacturing machinery	8,079	1,982	15	621	0	258	10,955
Males employed in retail trade, or handicraft, as masters or journeymen	4,012	623	1,305	215	126	171	6,452
Wholesale merchants, professional persons and other educated men.	758	233	114	68	1	33	1,234
Labourers employed by the three preceding classes, and in other labour, not agricultural.	1,731	198	243	69	24	440	2,640
All other males, 20 yrs. old (except servants) including retired Tradesmen, superannuated Labourers, & males diseased in body or mind	701	128	104	54	1	25	1,013
Males (servants) above twenty years of age.	30	46	6	10	7	0	99
Males (servants) under twenty years of age.	162	2	4	3	31	0	203
Females (servants)	1,214	414	237	186	25	79	2,165

RETURNS OF THE CENSUS OF 1841.

TOWNSHIPS.	Inhabited Houses.	Uninhbtd. Houses.	Houses Building	Males.	Females	TOTAL.
Attercliffe-cum-Darnall,	880	84	3	2,128	2,028	4,156
Ecclesall Bierlow	4,037	498	51	9,821	10,163	19,984
Brightside Bierlow....	2,065	250	18	4,931	5,158	10,089
Hallam (Nether)......	1,417	162	25	3,643	3,632	7,275
Hallam (Upper)	257	23	0	682	719	1,401
Sheffield	14,368	2,243	97	34,361	35,226	69,587
Total....	23,024	3,260	194	55,566	56,926	112,492

According to the foregoing table, the population has increased, within the last ten years, 20,800 ; the houses occupied, 4,691. The population of 1831 was 91,692, the houses occupied 18,331 ; which gives five inhabitants to a house. The returns of 1841 show the population to be 112,492, and the houses occupied 23,024. Smaller the proportion of inhabitants to the number of dwellings, and higher is the physical—the moral and the intellectual condition of the people. The fact is evidence of an ability in the mass to occupy separate houses, in place of several families being congregated together under the same roof, as in many manufacturing districts. There is another circumstance, also, worthy of attention. The houses un-inhabited in 1831—a period of depression, were 914 ; in 1841, 3,260 ; exceeding the former by 2,346. This fact might be brought forward in illustration of two different views : *as evidence of the effects of preceding temporary prosperity, or, as a measure of the existing distress.* The greater proportion of houses uninhabited in the one period than in the other, is chiefly to be ascribed to the extraordinary mania for building in 1835 and 1836. Speculation in this direction, was encouraged by circumstances which will be hereafter explained. The extravagant extent to which it was carried, will not be questioned. The same passion for building existed in the years 1824 and 1825, and property in consequence, as on the present occasion, became greatly depreciated in value. The uninhabited houses are, therefore, no exact measure of the prevailing distress. If such an opinion be urged, it may be stated that the number of inhabitants to the occupied houses is only a fraction less than in 1831, consequently as far as this fact goes, no deterioration, compared with that period, is exhibited in the condition of the population.

It would indeed scarcely be just to assume, that the population in the last decennial period, has increased at the same rate as in the preceding. The last comprises several years of severe commercial distress : 1831 and 1832 were times of great suffering ; and from autumn 1836 to the present moment,* we have had one uninterrupted season of ruinous distress. Thousands of artisans have been either out of employment, or receiving only a slender pittance for their labour.

In an inquiry of this kind, it is not altogether out of place, to record the causes of this protracted misery and struggling, as at some future time such facts may possess an historical value or interest. The years 1834, 1835 and 1836 were characterised by extraordinary prosperity. The demand for goods exceeded the power of production. The masters bade against each other in their offers to procure workmen, and wages, as a natural consequence, became extravagantly high. The spirit of enterprise manifested itself in the erection of new factories—in the extension of old establishments—in the formation of new streets, and

* January 2, 1843.

especially in the erection of elegant and imposing villas in the immediate neighbourhood. The universal passion was speculation. Joint Stock Banks were formed—in a few years no less than five in the town—which fiercely competed with each other for the privilege and honour of giving credit. Railways were projected, and capital flowed freely in this direction ; and many other undertakings of a purely speculative character, met with warm encouragement. While capital was thus spread over a greatly extended surface—was employed in new channels, the creation of manufactures exceeded the legitimate wants of the times, both in relation to home and foreign markets, and both, but especially the latter, by the middle of 1836, became thoroughly glutted.

Speculation was as rife in the United States, which are important markets for the productions of this town, as in this country, and insolvency, embarrassment and ruin were contemporaneous in both, and continue to be coexistent. The exports from this kingdom to the States, in the years 1835--6, will shew, more clearly than any remarks of ours, the extent to which the speculative spirit was carried.

1832................£5,468,272
1833................ 7,579,699
1834................ 6,344,989
1835................ 10,568,455
1836................ 12,425,605

The average value of the exports, for several years preceding 1835, was about £6,500,000, which in 1836 was nearly doubled, yet the panic occurred at the *beginning* of autumn, which, in a great measure, put a stop to commercial intercourse and enterprise.

We have unfortunately no means of determining accurately, the amount of the manufactures of the town, included
in the general exports of the country.   We should, however,
be disposed to claim for it, the greater part of the hardwares
and cutlery, of which the real value is stated in them, under
these respective heads.   An error in the estimate is of no
importance, as the exports of these articles are introduced
simply as an illustration of the fluctuations in the production of manufactures : an excess in a period of prosperity—
an excess in the subsequent and early stages of the depression, arising from struggles to overcome embarrassments,
and at length a greatly diminished amount, which, with
the ruinous cheapness of the articles, becomes a measure
of the existing distress.

EXPORTS OF HARDWARES AND CUTLERY IN THE FOLLOWING YEARS.

1833	£1,466,362
1834	1,485,233
1835	1,833,043
1836	2,271,313
1837	1,458,666
1838	1,498,327
1839	1,828,521
1840	1,345,881

In the year 1833 trade had become moderately good,
being the best year since the serious panic of 1825.   In
1834, prosperity, in its sober and healthy condition, was
general, and was imagined, at the time, as permanent in its
character.   The following year, 1835, was marked by wild
and speculative enterprises, and we perceive that the exports
rose from £1,485,233 to £1,833,043, and in the succeeding
year, when the panic occured, the exports had become
£2,271,313.   These figures are full of instruction to the
unprejudiced and reflecting.   The year succeeding the

panic, the exports were only £1,458,666. In 1839, without any improvement in the demand, they rose to £1,828,521, and this was occasioned by the exertions of the manufacturers, struggling to correct accumulating embarrassments. Immense quantities of goods were sent abroad on consignment, and sales were effected at a ruinous loss to the producers.

Poverty and misery are not favourable to a rapid growth of population.* They arrest the accelerated speed encouraged by prosperity. In taking the mean of the increase of the two preceding periods, 1811 to 1821, and 1821 to 1831, which is 2¾ per cent. per annum, it was proposed to determine the population of the town, and of the several townships comprising the parish. The procedure seemed calculated to afford pretty accurate results. The following table shows, according to this principle, the increase in the several townships, but which is shown, by the recent census, to be somewhat beyond the truth.

ESTIMATED POPULATION OF THE SEVERAL TOWNSHIPS COMPRISED IN THE PARISH OF SHEFFIELD, 1840.

TOWNSHIPS	Centesimal increase in 20 years, 1811 to 1831.	Centesimal increase per Annum.	Estimated Population, 1840.	Returns from the Registrar General's Office, 1841.
Sheffield...............	64¼	2½	73,856	69,587
Brightside Bierlow ...	83	3⁄10	11,772	10,089
Ecclesall Bierlow	117¾	3⁄10	20,263	19,984
Nether Hallam.........	95¾	3½	6,296	7,275
Upper Hallam.........	19½	0⁄10	1,121	1,401
Attercliffe-cum-Darnall	39⁄10	1⁄10	4,352	4,156
Total Estimated Population......			117,660	112,492

* This refers to the growth of the population from immigration.

D

INCREASE OF THE POPULATION FROM 1831 TO 1841.

TOWNSHIPS.	Real Increase from 1831 to 1841.	Increase per Centum, per Annum.	Population in 1841.*	Returns from Registrar General's offc Census 1841.
Sheffield..................	18	1¾	67,967	69,587
Brightside Bierlow ...	12¼	1¼	10,089	10,089
Ecclesall Bierlow	40	3½	20,005	19,984
Nether Hallam..........	59¼	4¾	7,275	7,275
Upper Hallam	85¼	3	1,399	1,401
Attercliffe-cum-Darnall	11	1	4,156	4,156
		Total...	110,891	112,492

The preceding table shows that the population has increased in very different proportions in the several townships. Ecclesall Bierlow and Nether Hallam exhibit great progress, while Attercliffe-cum-Darnall has advanced at a slow rate. These differences are easily accounted for. The immediate neighbourhood of the town, especially in the direction of Ecclesall Bierlow and Nether Hallam, is extremely beautiful, and offers numerous building sites of exquisite attraction. Wood, water and variety of scenery are its claims on the consideration of the affluent manufacturers—and the high hills and the quiet vallies have been enriched with elegant villas, displaying comfort—independence and taste. To this circumstance it is chiefly owing, that the rate of increase in the population has been greater in several of the townships than in others. The increase in Brightside Bierlow arises, however, from the extension of manufactures, and the many local changes which have taken place in it, as the making of new roads—the improvement of others, and the terminus of the Sheffield and Rotherham Railway. Some parts of this township

* These returns were published at the time of taking the Census by the Superintendent Registrar of this District.

present, also, many interesting sites for country residences, and which are beginning to be appreciated. The township of Attercliffe-cum-Darnall has no peculiar advantages for the purposes of manufacture, and few attractions to the builder, the greater part being flat and low. Upper Hallam is an exceedingly thinly populated district, difficult of access from the badness and ruggedness of the roads, and in all probability will increase very slowly.

The following table gives the Returns made to Government in 1838, by the Superintendent Registrar of this district; the general accuracy of which is unquestionable, indeed it has been confirmed by the census of 1841, and is presented as affording information on several matters of interest in relation to the town.

BOROUGH OR PARISH OF SHEFFIELD.

TOWNSHIPS.	Population.		Population beyond the Police Boundary.	County Rate. £.	Borough Voters.
	1831.	1838.			
Sheffield Township ...	59,011	72,000	500	111,216	2,482
Ecclesall Bierlow	14,279	17,500	2,500	29,016	847
Brightside Bierlow......	8,968	10,500	2,000	16,309	319
Nether Hallam	4,658	5,500	4,500	8,716	252
Attercliffe-cum-Darnall,	3,741	4,500	4,500	5,524	113
Upper Hallam	1,035	1,200	1,200	2,843	72
Totals......	91,692	111,200	15,200	173,624	4,085

The following table presents several interesting particulars, bearing on the condition of the town, during a lengthened period of uninterrupted distress. The payments to the casual poor, for four years, were comparatively insignificant—evidence of the exertions made by the artisan to maintain his independence.

FACTS, ELUCIDATING THE CONDITION OF THE TOWN, DURING SIX YEARS OF DISTRESS, FROM 1836 TO 1842.

Numbers in the Poor-House.		Annual Weekly Average Payments to regular Poor.		Annual Weekly Average Payments to casual Poor.	
		£.	s.	£.	s.
March, 1837	261	62	0	13	15
1838	401	65	0	39	0
1839	386	76	0	47	0
1840	443	77	0	50	0
1841	490	81	0	140	0
June, 1842	600	93	0	380	0
July,	471	100	0	461	0
Aug.	535	96	0	492	0
Sept.	511	102	0	468	0
Oct.	555	106	0	420	0
Nov.	615	102	0	420	0

	Total Payments to regular Poor.	To Casual Poor.	To Strange Poor in the Town.
March, 1836	£.	£.	£.
to 1837	3251	715	No.
1838	3390	2045	867
1839	3992	2460	820
1840	4017	2612	898
1841	4236	7315	1157
1842	4549	7244	1150

Year.	Paid for Flour, and Oatmeal.	House Department.	Total Expenses.
Ending March, 1837	£.	£.	£.
	760	2095	10,548
1838	1996	3734	14,084
1839	3121	4787	15,516
1840	3357	5368	18,065
1841	5237	7557	23,806
1842	4976	7242	23,716

This table contains several important facts to which we direct attention. Some persons are disposed to question the gradual improvement in the intelligence, morality and independence of the working classes. They look upon society as in a state of deterioration. We do not in any degree participate in such views. The many who have to labour are subject to extreme vicissitudes of trade—inordinate demand and corresponding depression, and hence are under the influence of forces which do not admit of steady and uninterrupted progress—the progress, however, is unquestionable. The intelligence of the masses in this manufacturing district, has made very obvious advances within the past twenty years. There is less tendency to lawless and violent proceedings—the understanding is more open to reason, and the different questions which agitate and interest the many, indicate, by their character and object, an improvement in the tone and views of the mind.

There is one column in the preceding table, the average weekly payments to the casual poor, which to us, familiar with the condition of the town, is exceedingly pleasing to contemplate. The commercial distress, almost unprecedented in degree, under which we are suffering began in 1836, not by imperceptible changes, but by a fearful panic, involving extensive embarrassments, and from this time to the present moment, the manufacturers have had to struggle against an uninterrupted series of difficulties. The diminution in the demand for labour was sudden, and at once felt by the artisans in almost every branch, and yet such were their independence and the resources on which they had to fall back, that they were years before the pressure of their necessities was felt by the parish. After four years of suffering, the average weekly payments were only £50. The value of this fact can be fully appreciated only by those, who have been intimately acquainted with the long and widely pervading wretchedness of the town. In former times, the rate-payers would have felt the pressure much earlier.

CHAPTER III.

COMPARISON BETWEEN THE PRESENT AND PAST PERIODS OF MANUFACTURING DISTRESS.

It is human nature to regard existing evils as far greater than any ever experienced. The present are felt—the past are remembered. The one is a matter of reality, and presents itself in painful associations with the views and calculations of the passing hour, and the anticipations of the future. Difficulties, especially if aggravated by years of suffering, gather around them imaginary hardships: the mind colours after the suggestions and struggles of the moment, and pictures an intensity of suffering out of all proportion with the substantial causes of it—actual privations and embarrassments.

This train of thought is suggested by the prevailing complaints of all classes, of the severe commercial depression existing; and they have indeed a real foundation; at the same time, it is possible to underrate past suffering and to exaggerate the present. With respect to this town, if we had no statistical details by which to measure past periods of manufacturing distress, we have monuments of them richly fraught with general truths—new roads constructed or improved by the unemployed artisans—grounds levelled or laid out, and other features of change. But the language which these speak is eloquent only to those whose recollection of such times is vivid, but particularly of the mode in which the suffering multitudes whiled away the tedious hours—bore the labours which were simply to test their necessitous condition. The following facts will give force to these truths, and are worthy of being recorded :

The subjoined table gives the population in different years,—the valuation on which the Poors' rate is collected, —payments for the County rate,—to the necessitous Poor,—the number of persons in the Poorhouse, and the cost per head; particulars important to record, and they will suggest a few remarks not altogether foreign to the inquiry.

Year ending Easter—	Population.	Valuation on which the Poor's Rate is collected.	Payments for the County Rate	Payments to out-poor viz. regular and casual Cases.	Number of Persons in the Poorhouse.	Cost per Head per Week.	
		£,	£,	£,		s.	D
1800	30,891	not known	177	7,200	not known	—	—
1805	33,081	———	107	9,589	———	—	—
1810	35,470	———	150	10,370	———	—	—
1815	38,075	44,200	195	9,449	———	—	—
1820	40,922	46,600	1,161	23,890	282†	3	3¼
1825	47,335	50,000	1,185	5,964	———	0	0
1830	57,565	55,000	1,415	7,080	334 incl.	2	10½
1831	59,011	56,500	1,675	6,757	319 —	2	11
1832	60,440	59,000	1,737	6,875	315 —	2	10
1833	61,981	61,500	1,519	8,692	374 —	2	9
1834	63,326	63,800	1,948	7,426	328 —	2	8½
1835	64,569	65,000	1,713	6,628	312 —	2	3½
1836	65,704	66,800	1,944	5,005	227 —	2	4
1837	66,725	71,520	1,712	4,065	252 —	2	6
1838	67,628	152,340	1,712	5,665	353 —	2	4
1839	68,408	157,240	1,196	6,400	349 —	2	7½
1840	69,062	159,200	2,430	6,587	352 —	2	8
1841	69,587	161,142	2,453	11,379	460 —	2	7
1842		162,965	2,575	11,627	469 —	2	7

† Exclusive of Gaol.

The proportions of the Rateable property, in the beginning of 1834, were as follows :—

Dwelling-Houses	£46,830
Manufactories and Mills	10,520
Land	4,410
Works and Tolls	700
Mines and Quarries	780
	£63,240

Taking the above *annual value*, however, in the aggregate, it was supposed not to amount to one-half of the *Rental*,—in fact the township, at that time, was assessed to the County rate in the sum of £111,216.

The houses on which the valuation of 46,830 was levied were of the following description :—

10,437 { at and under the real rental of £7 7s. 0d, valued at............ }	£21,375
1,160 above that sum, and under £10...	4,130
1,580 above £10, and under £20.........	9,200
652 upwards of £20........................	9,125
260 Public Houses	3,000
	£46,830

In one of the preceding tables, the payments to the out-poor is an important column, which cannot be passed over without a few remarks. It exhibits either extraordinary distress or gross mismanagement of the parochial affairs in past years.

In 1800, when the population was only 31,000, little more than one-third of the present amount, the payments to the out-poor were £7,200. In 1810, when the population was 35,00, they were 10,370 ; and in 1820, when the population was about half what it is now, they rose to the extraordinary amount of £23,890. Our recollections of this period are lively. The sufferings of the Rate-payers were indeed great. The *rental*, on which the Poor-rate was collected, was only £46,000, and almost one-half who ought to have contributed were either entirely inca-pacitated, or were not pressed for payment from a just apprehension that they would become chargeable to the town, consequently the burthen fell heavily on the few who were able to pay. It was common then for large placards to be posted, once or twice in the year, on the walls, as well as distributed among the rate-payers, containing the names of parties receiving parochial aid,—the trade,—the number of family, and the amount paid to them weekly. It will scarcely be believed, that some were receiving as much as 14s. and 15s. per week, and many from 8s. to 12s. with little enquiry into their circumstances. It was a notorious fact at the time, that many mis-called poor, were doing better than when trade was good. There was not only this mis-management with respect to the out-poor, but in every department of the parochial establishment. There was no system, economy, or consideration for the pockets of the rate-payers. There are not the same just grounds of complaints at the present time.

The following table gives the payments in corresponding weeks in the different years compared, from which it is evident, that if such data were admitted to be a measure of the distress existing at the respective periods, the present time does not stand out, characterized in a peculiar degree by prevailing suffering. The weekly payments to the casual poor in 1842, a year of greater embarrassment and misery than any of the five preceding, have not risen in the ratio of the increased population, compared with the payments of 1820. It may perhaps be said, and with some truth, that in the one period the public money was more lavishly distributed than in the other, so that the amount will not be a just indication of the proportion of the unemployed. We regard it, however, as a measure of the existing distress. If the recipients, at one period, were more liberally dealt with than at another, the rate-payers would necessarily be more heavily pressed, so that the weekly payments, in relation to the population, may be viewed as evidence of the embarrassment and wretchedness prevailing.

Weekly Payments to the Casual Poor, during the year commencing Easter, 1819, compared with those of the years commencing Easter, 1820 and 1842.

	1819.				1820.				1842.		
WEEKS.	L.	S.	D.	WEEKS.	L.	S.	D.	WEEKS.	L.	S.	D.
1	136	9	5	1	472	14	6	1	194	16	0
2	140	9	4	2	455	19	4	2	291	7	6
3	145	13	2	3	453	13	8	3	229	0	8
4	147	7	6	4	451	3	4	4	248	4	0
5	149	4	0	5	447	14	4	5	274	6	0
6	164	15	4	6	464	5	4	6	298	5	6
7	169	15	10	7	450	10	6	7	312	11	0
8	180	10	8	8	*436	7	4	8	333	14	6
9	191	0	10	9	437	8	6	9	359	12	6
10	196	11	0	10	436	14	4	10	347	9	0
11	215	5	1	11	425	18	6	11	368	8	6
12	215	4	6	12	433	3	10	12	371	17	6
13	221	10	6	13	414	1	0½	13	382	12	0
14	218	1	7	14	432	0	10	14	387	15	6
15	222	10	4	15	426	13	1½	15	398	16	0
16	229	12	4	16	412	19	2	16	424	12	6

* Employment being found for the paupers at the Park-Farm, and Clay-Wood, began to operate upon the payments.

	1819.				1820.				1842.		
WEEKS.	L.	s.	D.	WEEKS.	L.	s.	D.	WEEKS.	L.	s.	D.
17	248	16	2	...17	387	18	11	...17	441	5	6
18	265	7	3	...18	†354	8	2	...18	448	12	0
19	270	8	6	...19	345	7	4	...19	461	18	6
20	279	6	10	...20	332	4	2	...20	477	13	0
21	293	16	10	...21	316	1	4	...21	492	3	0
22	290	5	5	...22	298	14	8	...22	489	15	6
23	303	17	0	...23	294	3	0	...23	493	0	6
24	316	18	9½	...24	296	18	7	...24	496	3	6
25	314	4	3	...25	281	9	11	...25	503	10	6
26	302	16	6	...26	263	4	2	...26	503	10	6
27	311	10	3½	...27	247	9	8	...27	442	15	6
28	306	13	6	...28	256	6	9	...28	469	15	0
29	314	9	11	...29	250	8	2	...29	467	9	6
30	326	18	9	...30	‡217	0	10	...30	458	1	6
31	335	18	1	...31	213	8	0	...31	447	17	6
	£7,425	9	6		£11,406	11	4		£12,317	0	0

The population of the town in 1820 was 40,922; the sum paid to the casual poor in the 31 weeks commencing Easter, was £11,406. The population in 1841 was 69,587, and the sum paid to the casual poor in 31 corresponding weeks in the year following, was £12,317. In 1820, the amount of poor-rates collected was £34,109, in eight double books, making 6s. 8d. in the pound, on the rental: in 1842, £40,000, in five books, making 4s. 8d. in the pound on the rental, consequently the burthens were relatively much greater at the former than the latter period. Exertions were made then, as at the present time, to diminish the pressure on the rate-payers, and partial employment has generally been found in the making of roads—railways and projected improvements, affording some little relief.

† First week the plan of giving Certificates was acted upon.

‡ Reduced scale commenced this week.

At this time,* there are in the poorhouse 594 persons; and the township of Sheffield relieves out-poor of all ages, the extraordinary number. 6,488, more than one-eleventh of the whole population, among which number are able poor of the following occupations :

File cutters	113	89†
File grinders	8	17
File hardeners	4	1
File forgers	8	29
Spring knife cutlers	211	387
Pen and pocket blade forgers	14	26
Pen and pocket blade grinders	35	59
Table-blade forgers	18	22
Table-blade strikers	13	21
Table-blade grinders	22	30
Table-knife cutlers	84	168
Edge tool makers and strikers	21	16
Razorsmiths	21	22
Razor grinders	13	18
Fork makers	8	5
Fork grinders	16	9
Silversmiths	14	7
White metalsmiths	8	26
Moulders	7	4
Fender makers	6	4
Comb makers	6	8
Engine tenters	3	3
Saw handle makers	13	10
Saw makers	14	17
Scale cutters and pressers	20	39
Scissorsmiths	29	40
Labourers	59	66
Miscellaneous trades	134	129

* March 1, 1843.

† This column contains the able poor in July, 1842, after which time, about 200 found employment as excavators on the Manchester and Sheffield projected line of railway.

The scale of relief to the casual poor for six days' work is as follows :—

	IN MONEY. S. D.		BREAD. LBS.		SOUP. PINTS.
To a single man	1 6	...	9	...	3
— if married	2 0	...	12	...	4
— if one child	2 6	...	15	...	5
— if two children	3 0	...	18	...	6
— if three children	3 6	...	21	...	7
— if four children	4 0	...	24	...	8

Children above nine years of age are generally ordered into the workhouse school.

It would not be correct to ascribe the diminution of the poor-rates, compared with the population, altogether to a better system of management, enforcing stricter economy and a juster application of the funds. There is another cause which has co-operated with it, and to an extent much greater than is imagined by the public, viz.: *the accumulated resources of many branches of trade in union*. It is not our business, on this occasion, to point out the beneficial or injurious tendencies of combinations ; at the same time, it would be manifestly unjust to withhold facts. The funds of these branches are for the purpose of maintaining what they conceive to be remunerative wages. This is an object common to all. Another object, belonging to several, whose union is thoroughly established and in perfect operation, *is to relieve their own workmen out of employment*.

The internal arrangements of the poor-house exhibit system—economy—perfect cleanliness, and a regard to the feelings and habits of the aged and infirm, deserving the warmest commendation.

THE ORDINARY SIZE OF COTTAGE HOUSES IN SHEF-
FIELD.—Cottages usually contain each, a half cellar,—
sitting room or dining room, 12 feet square and 8½ feet
high, or 1224 cubic feet,—Chamber, 12 feet square, 8 feet
high, or 1152 cubic feet,—attic, 12 feet square, 7 feet high,
or 1008 cubic feet;—number of day rooms, one; of
sleeping rooms, two.

The artisans have usually an entire house for themselves,
and the cases are indeed rare in which two families are
found under the same roof. In Manchester, nearly twelve
per cent. of the population live in cellars; and in the
borough of Liverpool there is the immense number of
7,862 *inhabited* cellars. In this town we do not know of
one, and we are informed by the intelligent superintendent
of the police, that there is not an *inhabited cellar*. This
is somewhat remarkable. It would naturally be supposed,
that where the largest fortunes were accumulated, where
wealth in fact most abounded, the condition of the labouring
classes would be the most independent and comfortable.
Such, however, appears not to be the case. We have no
hesitation in asserting that the artisans here, as a body, are
vastly superior in intelligence, independence, and in the
command of the necessaries and luxuries of life to the same
class in the above-mentioned towns. We will not attempt
to account for results so little in harmony with the prevailing
opinion, on the necessary connexion between the creation
of wealth and the improvement in the condition of this all-
important class of producers. We question the connexion,
and regret that facts do not indisputably establish it.

CHAPTER IV.

AN INQUIRY INTO THE CAUSES OF UNOCCUPIED HOUSES.

In periods of commercial depression, numerous circumstances co-existing with distress, are seized as evidence of the faults or follies of legislation. Men seldom look near home for the causes of the evils under which they suffer. To trace them to their own conduct, is an effort to which few are equal. A season of depression always abounds in bad reasoning—bold assumptions, exaggerated statements and undefined grievances. The struggle to live, is always accompanied with the unscrupulous exercise of the privilege to complain. To presume to correct prevailing misconceptions—or to expose errors hugged with solicitude is a task which demands no ordinary independence.

That numerous houses are untenanted in manufacturing towns is an obvious fact; and co-existing with depression of trade, it is deemed equally manifest that the cause is the want of employment. Cause and effect in this instance are indissolubly associated in the minds of the many.

Living in the centre of a large manufacturing district, familiar with its localities, and the ever varying modifications in the enterprise of the capitalist—the extension and character of the staple manufactures carried on, and the numerous minor causes which influence the condition of the different classes of society ; and in addition, feeling no ordinary interest in the study of these objects, we enter upon the present inquiry, perhaps, with some little claim to consideration. To establish the correctness of our views we shall not go in search of illustrations beyond the precincts of this locality, though such procedure would not be without its value. We shall speak of facts which come within our own knowledge—of circumstances with which others are generally acquainted, and to win their assent to the arguments which they suggest, it is only necessary to analyse them.

The amount of unoccupied houses has been seized with avidity by parties, not only as evidence of the existing distress, but as an exact *measure* of it. It is a measure rather of previous prosperity than of commercial stagnation. It is no just indication of the latter. The amount, however, will always be somewhat proportionate to the existing depression, not because the one is the consequence of the other, which is the argument, but from both being effects of the same general causes. They are not to be viewed in relation to each other, strictly as cause and effect, but as having the same common origin—unrestrained and reckless over-production.

In a period of prosperity, the manufacturer is as little guided in the creation of productive power, by any natural demand, as the speculative builder is by the gradual augmentation of the population. They both equally neglect all calculations of the probable necessities of the future, enlightened by the data of the past. Neither acknow ledges the lessons of experience. The manufacturer feels the impulse of improved trade, and not only at once adapts his means to it, but concentrates both capital and credit to the enlargement of them; and every additional impulse calls into existence far more than a corresponding proportion of productive power. The demand, when on the advance, always carries the mind beyond it. The imagination is awakened, and the future presents itself in inexhaustible resources; and hence the invariable consequence of stimulated enterprise—glutted markets—the supply having overstepped the demand. If admitted that the productive power can exceed a legitimate demand, and this will scarcely be called in question, the surplus power thus created and unemployed in a period of depression, cannot certainly be referred to as a measure of the diminution of any natural demand; it is evidence not of existing distress, but of previous prosperity. The conduct, however, which led to the creation of this surplus power, produced, also, the depression of commerce, and thus misery and a vast amount of unemployed power always co-exist, but, clearly, to a considerable extent, as effects of the same general causes. The same reasoning will apply to the speculative builder. His actions are not regulated by the gradual increase of population, which, were it possible to ascertain it, would be the only just guide. In common with the manufacturer, he feels the impulse of improved demand, and the growing abundance of money necessarily directs a large amount of capital towards building objects;—hence the formation of new streets— the erection of houses, manufactories and public edifices.

E

A spirit of activity is observed in all directions. The town enlarges, and the immediate neighbourhood becomes studded with elegant and attractive villas; at length, however, the productive power becomes an ungovernable impulse, throws aside all sober restraint—all calculations as to the necessities of the population—a mania for building pervades all classes. New master builders spring up with questionable capital, and boldly project new streets. The houses erected letting either from their cheapness, or the desirableness of the situation, fresh means are acquired and especially credit to feed the speculative spirit: thus impulse added to impulse, creates, in the course of a few years, dwellings far exceeding the wants of the intoxicated times, and at last, the evils of the excess retard the rate of production.

The possibility of creating a surplus of houses will readily be admitted. If such exist contemporaneously with a period of commercial depression, with what propriety or justice can it be urged as the effect of it? The surplus, in general terms, has no connexion with the depression. It originated in prosperity, when speculative enterprise overleaped the boundaries of discretion and legitimate capital.

Independently of statistical evidence in corroboration of the fact, this must be obvious to all. Within the past few years, the town has extended widely in all directions. New roads and streets perplex by their variety; and astonishment seizes the contemplative mind in looking upon the vast creations around it. The same change presents itself in the picturesque sites of the immediate vicinity. There is no richly clothed hill or attractive valley, but what is embellished by the tasteful decorations of art.

The immediate neighbourhood gives evidence of new life, activity and happiness, and the changes in the picture have been effected chiefly within the past ten years. All classes, save the artisan and the needy shopkeeper, are attracted by country comfort and retirement. The attorney,—the manufacturer,—the grocer,—the draper,—the shoemaker and the tailor, fix their commanding residences on some beautiful site, and adorn them with the cultivated taste of the artist. We condemn not this relish for the quiet of country scenes, we adduce it simply as a fact which is familiar to all, and presented in no exaggerated colours. As an illustration of the truth of one part of the statement, we may mention, that in this town there are sixty-six attorneys, and generally men of high probity and respectability, and of this number, forty-one live in the country, and generally in the most costly mansions; and of the twenty-five remaining in the town, ten have been in practice only about five years. Were it necessary, similar particulars might be furnished with respect to the other classes of individuals alluded to, but the scope of this investigation does not require it. The fact shows, that while the town has been pressing on its prescribed limits, the country has gradually drawn from it, and, to a great extent, the wealthier part of the inhabitants. The immense production of houses on the one hand, and the stream of the population flowing into the country, on the other, satisfactorily account for the number of untenanted dwellings. In addition to these causes, the depression of trade tends to aggravate the general result, but the agency of it has been greatly exaggerated.

We proceed now to the examination of the circumstances which establish the correctness of our views. The number

of public and private roads or streets in the Borough, in
1840, was 386. The facts we shall present will show the
extent of the increase since 1831—what number has been
set out and made building land, and what number has
been projected. The table gives these facts from 1831 to
1836, and also from 1836 to 1841. The ten years are
divided into two equal periods, as each embraces, in some
degree, different conditions, the consideration of which is
important in this inquiry. In 1831, manufactures were
recovering from a long depressed condition, consequent on
the panic of 1825, and the improvement steadily increased
until the commencement of 1835, from which period to
the middle of 1836, speculation and overtrading exceeded
all previous bounds, and every class luxuriated in the
sunshine of temporary inflated prosperity. From 1836 to
1841 has been one uninterrupted series of suffering and
commercial embarrassment.*

TABLE SHEWING THE PROGRESS OF NEW STREETS IN THE BOROUGH
OF SHEFFIELD, FROM 1831 TO 1836.

TOWNSHIPS.	Entirely built.	Partly built.	Set out and made Building Land only.	Projected only.	Total.
Sheffield	4	29	23	20	76
Ecclesall Bierlow......	0	13	13	26	52
Brightside Bierlow ...	1	6	5	2	14
Attercliffe-cum-Darnall	0	1	1	0	2
Nether Hallam	0	6	5	1	12
Upper Hallam	0	0	0	0	0
Total......	5	55	47	49	156

These facts exhibit, with unerring fidelity, the speculative
spirit of the times. In the short space of five years, the

* This state of things, in its most aggravated form, exists at this
moment, March, 1843, and the numerous commercial failures in
the town, are evidence that it will continue some time.

new streets entirely built—partly built—set out and made
building land, and projected, amount to the extraordinary
number of one hundred and fifty-six, and independently
of the numerous erections in different parts of the town.
It is stated, in the second column, that fifty-six streets are
partly built. If the extension of building was at all regulated by the necessities of the population, it would naturally
be imagined that the fifty-six streets would have been
amply sufficient to satisfy such necessities; but while these
are only partially built, forty-seven are set out, and forty-
nine are projected.

THE FOLLOWING TABLE GIVES THE SAME PARTICULARS FROM
1836 TO 1841.

TOWNSHIPS.	Entirely built.	Partly built.	Set out and made Building Land only.	Projected only.	Total.
Sheffield...................	1	17	12	15	45
Ecclesall Bierlow	0	13	9	10	32
Brightside Bierlow ...	0	4	4	2	10
Attercliffe-cum-Darnall	0	0	0	0	0
Nether Hallam	0	6	0	0	6
Upper Hallam	0	0	0	0	0
Total......	1	40	25	27	93

The results of the latter five years are very different
from those of the former. Forty-five streets are partially
built, and the number set out twenty-five, while in the
first period there were forty-seven; the projected are only
twenty-seven, and of this number about thirteen are in
the Park District, the property of his Grace the Duke
of Norfolk. According to these tables the streets built—
partially built—set out as building land, and projected,
amount in ten years to two hundred and forty-nine. Will
it for one moment be doubted, after the consideration of
these facts, that a mania for building has been carried to a

reckless extent ?   Can evidence of a more satisfactory kind
be required in confirmation of the assertion ?   This vast
increase must have had a cause.   Was the gradual progress
of the population the cause ?   Certainly not.   It exceeded
the present and the immediately future wants of the population.   There was less sobriety of conduct exhibited
in the production of houses than in the extension of
manufactures.   Legislative interference cannot augment
the population to the unnatural supply of accommodation.
But suppose this accomplished, could the supply be maintained in harmony with the demand ?   Like causes always
produce like effects, and another fit of prosperity would be
accompanied with the same results.   The prospect of
present advantage throws an oblivious shade over the past,
and imparts an interest in the future only.   Like causes
with which the mind is enamoured, productive of evil, are
seldom contemplated as fraught with like consequences.
The understanding flatters itself with exceptions and the
kindly influence of undefined circumstances.

The new streets laid out or projected, are as just an
indication of the stirring passions of the times, as the
erection of houses.   The laying out, or the projection of
new streets, is the first step in the application of capital ;
and if no demand existed, the landowner or the capitalist
would not chalk out a field for future exertions and enterprise.   A street simply laid out yields no profit to the
owner.   He makes not a sacrifice of his land for the benefit
of the public, and, therefore, the fact is unexceptionable
evidence of the rampant spirit of speculation.

In the second table it is shown, that 40 streets were
partially built during the period of depression, when the

population would necessarily receive few additions from without—when the demand for dwellings was on the decline ; and the total built—set out, and projected, were 93. The spirit of enterprise cannot be arrested at once. Capital—credit—necessity or interest maintains it for a time, after the cessation of the primary invigorating power; and we have evidence of this in the continued extension of the town, when the demand for such extension no longer existed.

In confirmation of the tendency of the times to the over-production of houses, further evidence may be adduced. The following table is valuable from the particulars bearing on this subject. We regret that it is not in our power to present them for the whole parish, as in three of the townships, the increase of the population within the past ten years, and, consequently, cottage accommodation has been greater than in the township of Sheffield :—

TOWNSHIP OF SHEFFIELD.

TABLE SHOWING THE INCOME OF RATEABLE PROPERTY AND OF RATEABLE VALUE.

Rate for Highways when signed.	No. Pages.	Lines in each Page.	No. of entries	Amount at 6d. in the Pound.	Annual Rateable Value.	Increased annual val. in 9¼ years	Incresd. rateable items in 10 years	Increase of rateable items in 9¼ years
				£. s. D.	£. s. D.			
June 7th, 1831	594	28	16,632	2920 4 11¼	116,809 17 9¼	30 per cent.	nearly 50 per cent.	about 37½ per cent.
Jan. 1st. 1839	679	33	22,407	3874 8 2¼	154,976 7 6			
May 4th, 1841	705	33	23,265	3961 19 10¼	158,467 15 0			

These facts place beyond all doubt the immense increase, not only in the value of rateable property, but in the amount of rateable items. The distinction between the two is important. The value might possibly be greatly enhanced, from the expensive character of the buildings erected. The items have a reference to the number of them, hence are an accurate measure of the extension of building. The particulars given in each column are worthy of attention. They all confirm the same general conclusion. In $8\frac{1}{2}$ years, the annual value increased 30 per cent., and the rateable items, $37\frac{1}{2}$ per cent., and in ten years nearly 50 per cent. The items, in connexion with the augmentation of the population, are much more important than the value of the property, and the difference in this case between the two, shows that the tendency has been to produce houses of an inferior kind, and which are generally erected by the speculative builder. In our further researches, it will be fully established, that the mania for building has in no degree been regulated by the wants of the population.

This tendency to over-production is to be ascribed to three parties—the landowner—the petty capitalist—and the pennyless speculative builder. The first is naturally anxious to appropriate his land to building purposes, hence he sets it out in streets, or makes such roads as tempt the capitalist or the builder, either to purchase or to take on lease. The capitalist is desirous of realizing a handsome per centage, and this he endeavours to secure by the attractiveness of the situation and the cheap rate at which he builds.

During the period of commercial prosperity considerable demand for cottage accommodation existed, especially in districts possessing almost the advantages of the country, so that individuals, who could command only a few hundred pounds, were induced to erect numerous small houses. The calculation was to realize from 10 to 12 per cent., and this was frequently accomplished by the exceedingly slight and disgraceful character of the dwellings. An accurate description of the economical methods adopted—the ingenuity practised would scarcely be believed. In ordinary buildings, the bond timber which is inserted into the walls, is generally three inches thick, but in these modern structures, it is usually an inch, and occasionally not more than three-quarters of an inch. The joists, on which the floors rest, have only half the substance that is put into common houses, and is so contrived as to give the appearance of stability. The joists employed by the respectable builder are three inches thick, but the elaborate calculator of expense makes these into two, by sawing them in a diagonal direction, presenting to the observer who looks from below, a piece of timber two inches thick, when on the upper surface it is only one inch The same refined study to save material runs throughout the whole calculations.

The speculative builders never dream of the legitimate necessities of the population. The situation and style of the houses attract purchasers or tenants, when thousands are unoccupied, and thus encouragement to build co-exists with great commercial depression and an immense surplus of accommodation. These are startling truths, but in the further consideration of the subject they will be fully established.

The tendency to the over-production of cottage accommodation prevails largely at this moment,* as may be shewn by a particular case that falls under our immediate

* November 5th, 1841.

observation.   The street in which we reside is pleasantly
situate apart from the bustle of the town, and contains
twenty unoccupied dwellings.   In line with it commences a recently improved road, and the land on each
side is let for building purposes.   About twelve months
ago, a person erected nine houses on speculation, half of
which were untenanted until within a short time.   They
are now occupied with the exception of one.   A large
painted board states that they may be bought by private
contract.   Within the past few weeks, the same individual
has built eight others in continuation with the former, also
on speculation, when eight out of twenty-seven in the
same situation, and twenty in the adjoining street, are
untenanted !   ' Numerous facts of the same kind are observed
in every part of the town.

There is one speculator alone destitute of capital, who
has built 200 houses, not in the space of years, but almost
in the course of months, numbers of which are at present
untenanted.   As evidence of the general character of this
class of men, some of them actually cannot write their
names.

The mode in which these things are accomplished on a
large scale, is to get clay on the site fixed upon, and to
make bricks as long as the ground can be spared, or means
furnished by the forced sales of the property either partly
or wholly finished ; and on the completion of the undertaking, the projectors are often prepared to take the benefit
of the insolvent act, or fall into embarrassed circumstances,.
involving in their ruin many other parties.   The brick-
layer—the joiner—the glazier—and the painter frequently
combine their efforts—we can scarcely say their capital—

in extensive building speculations, and the existence of the whole body depends on a sale being effected, when the market is already glutted with cottage accommodation.

We proceed now to examine the returns of the census of 1831, which give the population—the number of inhabited and uninhabited houses; particulars which will throw much light on this inquiry.

CENSUS OF 1831.

TOWNSHIPS.	Population.	Inhabitd. Houses.	Uninhabited Houses.	No. of persons to each inhabited House.	Proportn. of uninhabited to inhabited Houses.
Sheffield..................	59,011	12,144	652	4.86	.054
Brightside Bierlow ...	8,968	1,790	41	5.01	.023
Attercliffe-cum-Darnall	3,741	784	25	4.77	.032
Ecclesall Bierlow......	14,279	2,519	136	5.67	.054
Nether Hallam.........	4,568	905	53	5.15	.059
Upper Hallam	1,035	189	7	5.48	.037
Whole Parish...	91,692	18,331	914	5.00	.050

According to these returns, the population was 91,692, and the inhabited houses 18,331, and the uninhabited 914. We have already remarked that trade in 1831, after a severe depression of nearly five years, was beginning to revive, perhaps, to a more manifest extent than at this moment. The circumstances of 1831 may, therefore, be compared with those of 1841.

The condition of the inhabitants of a town may, with considerable accuracy, be inferred from the proportion of individuals to each house. The more wretched the population, and greater is the proportion, each room being frequently occupied by single families. The more independent, and less the proportion. The returns of the population and of the inhabited houses, are consequently data of great value in this investigation. The foregoing table gives the number of persons to a house, in each township comprising the parish.

The average in the kingdom is stated by writers to be five. In two of the townships the number is less, and in the remaining four only slightly greater, and the aggregate returns for the six townships are exactly five persons.

THE FOLLOWING TABLE PRESENTS THE RETURNS OF THE

CENSUS OF 1841.

TOWNSHIPS.	Population.	Inhabitd. Houses.	Unin-inhabited Houses.	No. of persons to each inhabited House.	Proportn of unin-habited to inhabited Houses.
Sheffield..................	67,967*	14,101	2209	4.82	.157
Brightside Bierlow ...	10,089	2,064	250	4.89	.121
Attercliffe-cum-Darnall	4,156	880	84	4.72	.095
Ecclesall Bierlow	20,005	4,035	498	4.96	.121
Nether Hallam	7,275	1,416	159	5.14	.112
Upper Hallam	1,899	257	23	5.44	.090
Whole Parish...	110,891	22,753	3223	4.87	.142

Thus, in ten years, the population advanced from 91,692 to 110,891, the occupied houses from 18,331 to 22,753. The increase in the population being 19,199, in the occupied houses 4,422.

* The returns from the Registrar General's Office, not yet published, state the population of the township of Sheffield to be 69,587, making that of the whole parish 112,492.

The number of persons to each dwelling in the latter period, five years of which have been marked by commercial depression and unquestionable distress, is found, however, to be less than in 1831, not in one or two townships only, but in every township. This result was scarcely to have been anticipated. Our situation has been described as one of extreme wretchedness—as a breaking up of the elements of society—families that once occupied independent dwellings crowded into one house; and yet, when we analyze indisputable facts, we arrive at very different conclusions. In 1831, the average was five persons to each house; in 1841, 4.87. The number of uninhabited houses, in the former period, 914; in the latter, 3,223. So that, with fewer persons to each house than in 1831, the untenanted houses are greater by 2,309.

It may, perhaps, be imagined that the distress has caused numerous families to quit the town, and hence the immense surplus of cottage accommodation. '

We are prepared to show, that the emigration was greater in the five years preceding 1831, than in the five years preceding 1841. From 1820 to 1825 was a period of commercial prosperity, and contemporaneously of agricultural embarrassment. The town offered ample employment to the necessitous, and the native population was unequal to the demand. Crowds flocked from the country, impelled, on the one hand, by want; and, on the other, attracted by the abundance of labour. There never was a period when the immigration was greater than from 1820 to 1825, or when the population was increased more from without.

The following table gives the increase of the population
from 1821 to 1831, and from 1831 to 1841, and will be
found to corroborate the opinion we unhesitatingly express.

DECENNIAL INCREASE PER CENT., IN THE POPULATION.

TOWNSHIPS	1821 to 1831.	Annually.	1831 to 1841.	Annually.
Sheffield....................	40	3½	15¼	1½
Brightside Bierlow ...	35½	8	12½	1¼
Ecclesall Bierlow	56½	4½	40	3½
Attercliffe-cum-Darnall	18	1¾	11	1
Nether Hallam.........	42¾	3¼	59¼	4¾
Upper Hallam	1¾	0⅛	35¼	3
Whole Parish...	40½	3½	21	2

Thus, in the first ten years, the whole parish increased
40½ per cent., and in the latter, 21 per cent., or annually
3½ per cent., and about 2 per cent.   The aggregate annual
increase in the whole kingdom is nearly 1½ per cent.
Greater the augmentation in the period of prosperity, and
greater would be the emigration in the subsequent period
of adversity; or the less native the character of the population, and greater the subsequent changes; the new
elements having ties and attractions without, which, in a
season of suffering and misery would gradually draw them
from the centre towards the circumference, or in directions
whence they had migrated; and the fact was insisted upon
at that time precisely as at this moment.   If it had any
value then, it has the same value now, and we admit it in
both cases, assigning reasons, however, for the emigration
being greater previously to 1831 than 1841.   The varying
ratios in the increase of the population at different periods,
are frequently adduced to show the injurious effects of
narrow and unjust principles of legislation, as if the utmost

freedom of commerce could possibly prevent fluctuations in
trade. A lengthened season of prosperity, imparts a rapid
impulse to the increase of population in towns, by promoting marriages and immigration. A lengthened season
of adversity, at once retards the ratio of the increase.

The following table presents the progress of the population, within different periods, for more than a century, and
shows how exceedingly variable it has been in the township
of Sheffield :—

Years.	Houses.	Inhabitants.	Inhabitants to each House.	Increase per Cent.
1736	2,152	9,695	4.51	in 19 years 24
1755	2,667	12,001	4.50	in 33 years 109½
1788	6,161	25,141	4.08	in 8 years 15¼
1796	7,657	29,013	3.79	in 5 years 8
1801	7,720	31,314	4.05	in 10 years 14½
1811	7,927	35,840	4.50	in 10 years 17½
1821	10,036	42,157	4.20	in 10 years 40
1831	12,144	59,011	4.86	in 10 years 15¼
1841	14,101	69,587	4.93	

It is evident from these facts, that the population has
advanced by fits, and such must inevitably be the case
from fluctuations in commerce. In the fourth column, the
number of inhabitants to each house is given. The returns
for the first five periods cannot, however, be depended upon,
the unoccupied being included in the gross number of
houses, which in the subsequent calculations are excluded.

The increase of the population in the whole parish for
the past ten years has been 21 per cent., little more than
half the amount of increase in the preceding ten, and yet,
in the latter period, the increase in the rateable value of
property, and in the number of rateable items, has exceeded

the ratio of the augmented population from 1821 to 1831, clearly establishing an extraordinary degree of speculative building.

The prevailing doctrine is, that untenanted houses arise from two causes—emigration from the town and the crowding of families into one house. We have set at rest the latter argument, by proving that there are fewer persons living in each house than in 1831. If we admit the former, viz., an extraordinary amount of emigration, it will scarcely be contended, that co-existing with it *there can be any necessity for the creation of additional cottage accommodation.* And yet, in the past 3½ years of severe commercial depression, the tendency to further production has continued. While the inhabitants are stated to be quitting their dwellings, unable to maintain them, the speculative builder has been busily employed. In the parish of Sheffield, in 3½ years, the subjoined number of houses was erected :—

HOUSES ERECTED IN THE BOROUGH OF SHEFFIELD IN THE FOLLOWING YEARS.

TOWNSHIPS.	1838.	1839.	1840.	HALF 1841.	TOTAL.
Sheffield Township ...	359	586	225	188	1358
Brightside Bierlow......	45*	45*	48	50	188
Ecclesall Bierlow	176	132	126	65	499
Attercliffe-cum-Darnall,	3	8	10	7	28
Nether Hallam	123	189	67	50	429
Upper Hallam	10	10	10	5†	35
Totals......	716	970	486	365	2537

* The number of houses returned was ninety for these two years

† The increase stated to be about ten houses per annum. The particulars not given for each year.

These facts are alone sufficient to prove the reckless spirit of the times. In 3½ years, during which manufactures have been exceedingly depressed, and while indeed numerous families it is stated have emigrated, the cottage accommodation created, in reckoning five persons to each dwelling, which is about the average, would meet the necessities of an additional population of 12,685—a rate of increase at least double what occurred in the most extraordinary season of commercial prosperity. The population from 1821 to 1831 was marked by greater progress than at any other period, and yet during these ten years, the increase was only 16,854; whereas if the population had advanced in the past ten years, *in the ratio of the building within the last 3¼ years* of great commercial suffering, the actual increase would have been nearly 38,055.

Every step in this investigation establishes the over-production of dwellings. In 1831, the houses unoccupied were 914, and as these were ready to supply the growing necessities of the population, philosophically viewed, they are to be regarded as houses created within the past ten years; for if the extension of building was at all regulated by the wants of the population, it is manifest that the untenanted houses would be first occupied; this number is, therefore, to be added to the houses actually created within the period. If the 914 be added to the 6,731, built within the past ten years, we have a total of 7,645 houses; and if the population had increased in the ratio of the accommodation, the augmentation would have been 38,225, whereas it was only 19,026. Can it, therefore, be a matter of surprise that the number of houses should far exceed the necessities of the population? The population in-

F

creased in the period 21 per cent., but if it had advanced
in the proportion of the dwellings, the progress would
have been at the rate of nearly 42 per cent. It has been
stated, in answer to these facts, that the builders took into
consideration the increase of population in the preceding
ten years, which was 40½ per cent., and, consequently, they
calculated on the same progress in the following ten years.
Even admitting the argument, it proves all that we contend
for, viz., over-production. According to this argument,
the builders, like the manufacturers, are acknowledged to
have created houses, not in harmony with any existing
demand, but in the anticipation that such would occur in
extent equal to the speculation.

The class of builders, however, who have been instru-
mental in the creation of surplus accommodation, cannot
certainly be complimented with looking far back for data
to regulate their conduct. Their education and position
in society do not enable them to make fine calculations.
As already remarked, many of them cannot write their
own names, and the majority are not one remove from
condition of journeymen.

Is there not, indeed, a certain degree of absurdity in
imagining an increase of population in every subsequent
ten years, in the ratio of that which occurred under
extraordinary circumstances—during a vast extension of
trade, which attracted both capital and labourers from
other districts ? There must be some limits to the markets
both at home and abroad, and in order that the population
may increase 40½ per cent., the demand for goods must
increase in a greater ratio, or, in all probability, the condition of the masses would be greatly deteriorated.

From the preceding facts it is manifest, that the actual necessities of the inhabitants have exercised no sober control over the speculative spirit. Is it possible for any conclusion to be more satisfactorily established? The arguments throughout the investigation are based upon data, the general accuracy of which will not be questioned.

May we not, therefore, assert, that not only during a period of commercial prosperity was building carried to a ruinous extent, but even in a season of painful and protracted adversity? With what propriety then, can the number of untenanted houses be adduced as evidence of existing distress, being clearly a measure of the speculative enterprise which had previously animated all parties?

This speculation in building has produced the common effects of speculation—a cheapening in the article created, and to an extent that will scarcely be credited. Houses and buildings generally have fallen in value, within the past five years, at least 25 per cent. High authorities state it at 30 per cent., and were such property to be estimated at what it would sell for at this moment, which, of course, is the only measure of its value, the reduction would exceed what is here stated.

This reduction in value exercises less influence on the creation of new houses, than it would in the production of articles generally. When the farmer has seriously cheapened his grain by the excess grown, he quickly corrects his error: but the builder, when an immense surplus of dwellings already exists, finds employment by gratifying the taste of the purchaser or tenant, in the superior advantages of site, such as convenience, beauty

F 2

or healthiness ; and; therefore, as long as the situations selected are attractive, or the houses tempting from their accommodation and style, he acquires, at every step of his progress, resources for future exertions. The fact that thousands are unoccupied makes little impression upon him. His study is to please the eye at a cheap rate, and he is exceedingly successful in his efforts.

CHAPTER V.

COMPARISON OF THE COTTAGE ACCOMMODATION IN SHEFFIELD WITH THAT IN OTHER MANUFACTURING TOWNS.

We have already remarked, that the manufactures of this town can be carried on with advantage with a small capital, hence the numerous small masters in every branch, and the consequent competition. This circumstance is not without its beneficial effects. The absence of a few large fortunes is more than compensated by the much greater proportion of the middle classes, and the higher condition of the artisans, than in districts where the few are the monopolisers of wealth. The influence of this circumstance is observed, in a marked degree, in the character of the cottage accommodation in this town. Here families are not crowded into one house, as in Manchester, Liverpool, Bolton, Stockport and Rochdale, but each has generally an independent or entire dwelling; nor are the houses so constructed, that the only ingress to them is a narrow alley, or a confined cul-de-sac. They either front streets, or open into moderately spacious yards.

We shall proceed to show the ratio of the cottage accommodation to the population, in each of the townships of Sheffield, and in several important manufacturing districts. The calculations are founded on accurate statistical returns made to Parliament. The number of houses occupied, empty and building, and the existing population, in several of the undermentioned districts for 1831, are the only elements wanting to complete the view.

IN THE PARISH OF SHEFFIELD, 1841.

Inhabited houses to 1,000 residents 205
Empty do. 29
Building do. 1.72

235.72

TOWNSHIP OF SHEFFIELD, 1841.

Inhabited houses to 1,000 residents 206
Empty do. 32
Building do. 1.39

239.39

The number building is so small, that the reader had better leave out the decimal point, and regard the 172 and 139, as representing the houses being erected to 100,000 inhabitants, which of course is the proportion.

COMPARISON OF THE COTTAGE ACCOMMODATION IN THE SEVERAL TOWNSHIPS OF SHEFFIELD TO 1000 INHABITANTS.

TOWNSHIPS.	Inhabited Houses.		Empty Houses.		Houses Preparing.	
	1831	1841	1831	1841	1831	1841
Sheffield..................	206	206	11	32	4.51	1.39
Ecclesall Bierlow......	176	202	10	25	11.55	2.50
Brightside Bierlow ...	200	205	5	22	0 10	1.78
Nether Hallam	194	195	11	22	5 58	3.44
Upper Hallam	183	183	7	16	0.97	0.00
Attercliffe-cum-Darnall	210	212	7	20	0.27	0.72
Total Parish...	200	205	10	29	5.10	1.72

From these facts it is evident, that at the last census, (1841,) there were fewer individuals to each house, or, in other words, more houses occupied to every 1,000 inhabitants than in 1831, which would indicate an improvement in the social condition of the population. We observe very different proportions in England and Scotland generally, and, also, in the great manufacturing towns, where the few accumulate immense fortunes; and from such differences alone, we should infer, which is the fact, a much more degraded condition of the labouring classes. The machine not only enriches the monopolist of wealth, but creates, at the same time, a large amount of wretchedness, suffering and disease.

NUMBER OF HOUSES INHABITED, UNOCCUPIED AND BUILDING TO 1000 OF THE POPULATION.

	Inhabited Houses.		Unoccupied Houses.		Building.	
	1831	1841	1831	1841	1831	1841
England	178	184	9	11	1.80	1.73
Scotland	156	191	5	9	1.09	1.05
Lancashire	171	173	8	14	2.12	2.30
Bolton	—	185	—	23	—	0.53
Liverpool	—	148	—	4	—	2.10
Manchester	—	168	—	14	—	0.89
Rochdale	—	185	—	25	—	1.48

The particulars respecting these towns are incomplete; they are given only in reference to the latter period, 1841. But how marked is the difference, in the social condition of the population in Liverpool and Manchester, as indicated by these facts, compared with Sheffield! Every 1,000 inhabitants in Liverpool are living in fewer houses by 57, and in Manchester by 37, than the population of this town, so that in the former place, there are nearly seven persons to each house, in the latter nearly six, and in Sheffield about five. In general terms, there are in Liverpool 700 persons to every 100 houses—in Manchester 600, and in this town 500. These different proportions have corresponding degrees of wretchedness and disease.

The foregoing facts are also evidence of the speculation in building. In the parish of Sheffield, in 1831, when there were five persons to each house, 11 dwellings to 1,000 inhabitants were unoccupied; in 1841, when there were not five persons to each house, 29 dwellings to every 1,000 of the population were untenanted, so that accommodation had been created in ten years, *beyond the growing necessities of the town,* equal to 16,115 inhabitants. The population *had* increased, within this period, from 91,692 to 112,492, and while, in 1841, there were fewer persons to each house than in 1831, the surplus cottage room was equal to the wants of 16,115 additional inhabitants. In England, the difference in the number of the unoccupied houses between the two periods was only two dwellings to the 1,000 inhabitants—in Scotland four, in Lancashire six, but in Sheffield 18; and in accordance with these facts, we find that in this town, the number of unoccupied houses, in 1841, was far greater than in Liverpool, Manchester, Rochdale or Bolton, and yet, the distress of the labouring classes has been unquestionably less here than in any of these places.

CHAPTER VI.

THE SURFACE AND SUB-CONDITION OF THE STREETS IN THE TOWNSHIP OF SHEFFIELD.

The following Report on the state of the Roads in the Township of Sheffield, includes not only particulars concerning the surface and sub-condition, but several tables and much valuable information respecting the extent and cost of the roads, and likewise an account of various improvements in the making and repairing of them, which are highly worthy of attention.

For convenient reference, the present condition of the roads has been taken in districts. The collecting divisions for the Poor and Highway Rates are not alike, and the boundary lines are so arbitrary as frequently to divide streets and even the same premises. The Registration Districts have therefore been made use of, as affording a fair and tolerably equal division of the township.

These districts are four in number: the point from which they radiate is the Lady's Bridge. The PARK DISTRICT includes all the roads in the township South-east of the River Sheaf. The SOUTH DISTRICT is bounded by the

Sheaf and Waingate, Castle-street, Angel-street, High-
street, Fargate, Coalpit-lane, Porter-street, and Brammall
lane.   The WEST DISTRICT joins the above, and is bounded
by Bridge-street, Newhall-street, Westbar, Westbar-green,
Tenter-street, and Broad-lane.   The NORTH DISTRICT
joins the West, and is bounded by the division line of the
townships in Watery-lane, Portmahon, the Infirmary, Philadelphia and the river Don.

From such a division of the town, correct and valuable
data for future comparison will be obtained. By giving
the number and extent of highways and roads in each
district, as in Tables I. and II., the subsequent extension
of any district may at once be ascertained—the increased
liability of the township to repair them—the public or
private improvements effected—or any deterioration in
their condition may be remarked.

It is not necessary to dwell on the advantage of good
roads, or of the importance of a perfect system of sewerage,
where large masses of people are congregated together.
Nothing can contribute more to the comfort and convenience of the public, than *firm, dry* and even roads; or be
more conducive to health than efficient sewers, by which
the refuse of a large town may be immediately removed.

There are probably few towns better situated for natural
drainage than Sheffield; in one part only does water falling
from the clouds remain, viz.: Shales moor, Spring-street,
Norris-field, &c., in the North district. The undulating
surface of the town is, in some respects, a disadvantage to
the inhabitants, but fully compensated by its generally
dry state.

Tables I. and II. exhibit many private roads, some of which cannot properly be called streets, but are taken into account, being open to the public, and from the owners being liable to contribute, in the ratio of their property in such situations, towards the repairs of them. The private roads do not demand any lengthened notice, with few exceptions, being back-lanes or bye-paths, little used and not known beyond their locality, unless they belong to the Church Burgesses, Town Trustees, or some other public body, or to his Grace the Duke of Norfolk, the Lord of the manor. They are usually in a very bad condition. In some cases, whole streets of cottage property have been built on speculation, making only a footpath of inferior flags, to render the houses just tenantable, the streets being allowed to remain in the most neglected state, exhibiting the accumulation of rubbish and filth of every description, and also stagnant pools of water, which in summer are offensive and injurious to health.*

These evils have been aggravated since the passing of the general highway act. Surveyors formerly repaired the streets in which they had a personal interest, and paved such private roads as were thought of importance to the public, on the owners of the property agreeing to pay half the expense. The owners of roads not belonging to the public are now expected to pay the whole of such cost, and to put them in such a condition as will be satisfactory to two justices of the peace and the surveyors.

The avarice or obstinacy of one owner frequently prevents the necessary improvements being carried into effect, and whole streets, in consequence are left in an unfinished state.

* Leicester-street, Carr-lane, and the lower part of Duke-street, Brown-street, until lately, School-lane, Park, &c.

The more liberal owners who may have repaired their portion are compelled to keep possession of it until the whole street is completed as required by act of Parliament. Such has been the reluctance of the owners of property to do what is best calculated to promote their own interests, that the town has become liable to repair one new road only since the commencement of the year 1836.

In speaking generally of the public sewers of the town, it may be remarked that many are not sufficiently capacious for the necessities of the district. They were planned and executed according to the direction of the surveyors for the time, who were gentlemen in office only for one year, without due regard to level, section, or the peculiarities of the locality. During the last nine years, many of the sewers have been enlarged, and all the new ones have been made sufficiently capacious to allow persons, without inconvenience to repair and cleanse them. It will be seen, by reference to Table I., that the total number of public sewers is 127, and the aggregate length, as shown by Table II. is 10 miles, 3 furlongs and 25 poles. The longest line is from Portobello, near the top of Gell-street, to Lady's bridge, being 1650 yards : the second in extent is 1320 yards, proceeding from Portmahon and terminating at the last mentioned place.

In situations where the inclination of the road was great, soughs, protected by street grates, were formerly made. These are not designated " common sewers," nor are they taken at all into account in this report, partaking only of the nature of covered channels. With about four exceptions,* there is a very marked inferiority in the private compared

* St. Philip's-road, Dixon-street, New Queen-street, and Matilda-street,

with the public sewers. The private sewers are 26 in number, and altogether extend 1 mile and 1331 yards. They are nearly all branch sewers, falling into the common sewers of the town.

Many of the private sewers are of small dimensions, without sheeting stones at the bottom, so that, after the lapse of a few years, the soil is washed away from beneath the walls, and the whole structure falls in.

The following table shows the number, the quality and the condition of the roads in each district, public and private: the number of streets having public or private sewers, wholly or in part: the number of roads without sewers, and the amount of the Highway rate in each district at 6d. in the pound, being the sum levied.

By referring to the number and extent of roads in each district repaired or paved, with the several descriptions of material used, distinguishing the good and bad of each, a pretty accurate opinion may be formed respecting the condition of the whole, or any part of the town.

The term " *Good*" is applied to the condition of the surface; and has reference to a road paved with square stones, in as excellent a state as the Old Haymarket; to one set with boulders in the condition, of High-street, Park; and to a road macadamized, in the state of Shrewsbury-road.

The term "Bad," as to square stones, will apply to Church-street ;—as to boulders, to Old-street, *Park district;* to Red-croft and Orchard-lane, *West District ;* and to Radford-street and Cupola-street, *North District ;*—and as applied to macadamised roads, the word " Bad" would attach to " Crown-alley, *Park District,* and the upper part of Portobello, in the *West District.*

TABLE I

DISTRICT	ROADS													SEWERS							RATES
	Condition as to Surface of Public Roads.						Condition as to Surface of Private Roads.				Total Public Roads.	Total Private Roads.	Total Roads.	Public.			Private.			Roads not Sewered.	Amount of the Highway Rate at Sixpence in the Pound.
	Square Stones		Boulders.		Macadamized		Wholly Private.		Partly Private.					Wholly Sewered.	Partly Sewered.	Total.	Wholly Sewered.	Partly Sewered.	Total.		£. s. d.
	Good.	Bad.	Good.	Bad.	Good.	Bad.	Good.	Bad.	Good.	Bad.											
Park.....	4	0	16	1	15	4	16	16	1	1	40	34	74	1	2	3	1	2	3	68	689 11 0¾
South ...	27	0	24	2	5	0	6	14	2	1	59	23	82	17	11	28	6	3	9	45	877 14 9¾
West.....	81¼	1	40½	2	6	1	14	18	2	0	81	34	115	35	11	46	2	4	6	63	1316 10 5¼
North...	15¼	0	59¼	2	5	0	6	27	0	1	82	84	116	30*	20	50	5	3	8	59	1078 0 6
Total...	78	1	140	7	31	5	42	75	5	3	262	125	387	83	44	127	14	12	26	235	3961 16 9¾

* One Street in this District has two Common Sewers.

Table I. does not alone present a sufficiently clear view of the superficial state of the town, because one road, or one common sewer, may be ten times as long as another. To afford still further information, the following table is added, shewing the length, in each district of the various descriptions of public and private roads, and of public and private sewerage, in chains and miles.

TABLE II.

District.	Extent of various kinds of Road, in Chains.					Extent of Sewerage in Chains		
	Square Stones.	Boulders	Maca-damis.	Total Public.	Total Private.	Public Sewers.	Private Sewers.	Total.
	CH. LK.	CH. LK.	CH. LK.	CH. LK.	CH. LK.	CH. LK.	CH. LK.	CH. LK.
Park.....	29 50	178 00	326 75	534 25	719 50	40 50	15 50	56 00
South....	227 50	299 00	76 00	602 50	170 50	194 50	42 50	237 00
West.....	206 50	262 00	69 50	538 00	145 00	281 25	35 00	316 25
North....	139 00	494 50	71 75	705 00	161 00	320 00	47 50	367 50
Total Chns.	602 50	1233 50	543 75	2379 75	1296 00	836 25	140 50	976 75
Total Miles Furlongs & Poles......	M. F. P. 7 4 10	M. F. P. 15 3 14	M.F.P. 6 6 15	M. F. P. 29 5 39	M. F. P. 16 1 24	M. F. P. 10 3 25	M. F. P. 1 6 2	M. F. P. 12 1 27

Table I., shews that though the roads in the Park are fewer in number, and the amount of the Highway rate considerably less than in any other district, the roads, public and private, are equal in extent to one-third of the whole; and, also, that though the roads paved with square stones, in the West District, are rather more in number than those similarly paved in the South; the latter exceeds the former in extent. The total length of public and private roads in the township of Sheffield is very nearly 46 miles; of public roads, by which is always understood those repaired and paid for by the town, a little less than 30 miles; and the public sewerage is about 10½ miles in length. The roads repaired by the town are in number 262, and the total number of public sewers is 127. More than one-third, therefore, in *number* and *extent,* are provided with

common sewers, which is believed to be a greater proportion
than is found in most large towns.   It may be fairly
presumed, that the artificial drainage of this town is comparatively efficient and adequate to the wants of a large
population.

In the Park District, there are many private roads of considerable length ; some leading to the farms are in a very bad
condition.   The greater part of those intended for streets are
newly formed by the auditor of the Duke of Norfolk,* and
many of them, in every respect, are equal to the public roads.
It will be seen by this table, that the Park District is almost
destitute of sewers, either public or private, but such is the
inclination of the surface, that in a few minutes, after the
heaviest thunder storm, the whole of the water which may
have fallen entirely disappears.   Some improvement in the
sewerage, however, is desirable, and will no doubt, ere long,
be effected.   About £200 were expended in the year 1839,
in completing the common sewer in Broad-street, on a
sufficiently large scale to form a trunk, to which branches
might be conducted to drain the whole of that part of the
district, which is densely populous.   There is perhaps a
larger amount of heavy *down traffic* on the Park road than
on any road within fifty miles.   The gradient of it is one
in twenty-two.   It is rather more than 1¾ mile in length,
and with every facility for obtaining good material at a
cheap rate, it costs annually, taking the average of four
years, about £1450, which is more than twopence in the
pound on all rateable property in the township, or one-
sixth of the amount expended on all the common sewers

* Michael Ellison, Esq.

and public highways.* Duke-street, Park, is on the same
line as the Park road, having also the same gradient, and
there was, during that period, about-equal traffic upon it ;
but it is paved with boulders.

TABLE III.

THE FOLLOWING TABLE SHOWS THE COST OF MAINTAINING EACH
IN A GOOD STATE OF REPAIR.

	Length.	Matrl.	1836-7.	1837-8.	1838-9.	1739-40.	Average per Year.	Cost per Mile, per Annum.
Park Road	1¾ miles and 12 poles. or 3146 yds.	Ganister and Lime-stone.	£. s. d. 1357 12 8	£. s. d. 1266 2 0	£. s. d. 1279 14 11½	£. s. d. 1894 15 0	£. s. d. 1449 11 1¾	£. s. d. 810 18 9¾
Duke st. 600 yards		Boldrs	64 6 6	40 9 4	52 10 8	46 4 1½	50 17 7¾	149 5 1½

Facts cannot more decisively prove the comparative
economy of paved over macadamized roads. A road paved
with square stones, all other circumstances being similar
to the above, would cost less annually, by £400 per mile,
than if macadamised. In consequence of these results
established by experiment, many of the great thoroughfares,
previously macadamized, have been lately paved with square
stones, the consumption of which, in the year 1836-7, being
about 8,000 yards; and in 1837-8, about 7,000 ; 1838-9,
about 8,500; 1839-40, about 7,700; 1840-1, about 4,000;
and in 1841-2, about 4,500 yards. The public are now
feeling the benefit of such an outlay, in the reduction of
the highway-rate, which took place a year and a half since,
from *eightpence* to *sixpence* in the pound.

* On Friday, October 16th, 1840, the least busy day in the week,
and during a state of great depression in trade, there passed upon
this road, between the hours of five in the morning and seven in
the evening, 1040 vehicles, chiefly used for the conveyance of coals.

The *South District*, as already remarked, contains a larger proportion of roads paved with square stones than any other district; and on reference to the tables, it will be found, that though the number is much less than in the West, the extent of public and private roads is greater. Those which are classed as "*bad*," though not of any great importance as thoroughfares, are admitted to be very injurious to the health of the neighbourhood. Some are almost in the condition of dung-hills during the greater part of the year. With respect to sewerage, the district is deficient as compared with the *West* or the *North*, which is partly owing to the natural inclination of the surface. Some of the streets have a direction nearly at right angles to the line of the river, as Sycamore-street, Howard-street, Charles-street, Furnival-street, Duke-street, and these have public sewers; while others, as Eyre-street, Arundel-street and the adjacent lanes fall in a direction contrary to but parallel with that of the river, and are therefore drained only at the points of intersection with the streets previously named. The sewerage of this district is nevertheless much better than it was a few years ago—public sewers having been made in Union-street, Pinstone-street, New Church-street, Norfolk-row, Sycamore-street, and other places. There is scarcely any part of the town where a common sewer is more required than in Surrey-street, which, being nearly level from Norfolk-street to the Music-Hall, it is almost impossible to remove the surface water. By making a sewer from Sycamore-street along Tudor-street, or one from Howard-street, along Arundel-street, to Surrey-street, which is of great importance, it might be effectually drained.

The *West District*, though containing, with the exception of the *North*, the greatest number of roads, will, on reference to the table, be found to be the least in superficial extent. It is limited on the West by the boundary line of the townships of Nether Hallam and Ecclesall Bierlow. The amount of its contribution towards the repair of the roads is considerably greater than that of any other district, hence it is obviously the most densely populated. The upper part of it is, perhaps, as respectable as any portion of the town. The lower abounds, however, in confined courts, filthy dwellings, and the most depraved part of the population. To persons at all acquainted with the town, in corroboration of these remarks, it is sufficient to name Castle-green, Water-lane, Scargill-croft, New-street, Red-croft, and many of the courts and bye lanes in the vicinity; Holly-street; Bailey-field,—a street about 150 yards in length, and yet containing more than 40 workshops and 192 houses, 134 of which are in close and unhealthy courts, and many of them are occupied by the lowest class of artisans and Irish. They are the resort of thieves and prostitutes. Taking the inhabitants of Bailey-street at five per house, which is greatly beneath the truth in property of this description, and allowing merely one person for each workshop, the population of this street only is 1000.*

Many of the private roads are in the condition of those just described, being short bye-roads, and never repaired, except by throwing ashes into the ruts and holes, by which means they are raised considerably above their original level, and are both disgusting and injurious to the health of the neighbourhood. There are in this district some exceptions: Watson walk, a private road, is well

* There is no public sewer in Bailey-field, and most of the court yards are below the level of the street. The street however is well paved.

paved and flagged : the same may be said of Victoria-street, the property of the Bath Building Company.

The public roads in this district will be greatly improved by carrying into effect certain plans, for which an Act of Parliament was, a few years since, obtained by the Town Trustees ; such as opening a communication between the old part of Queen-street and Westbar-green, and the widening of Holly-street ;* the widening of Snig-hill, Campo-lane, and Trippet-lane, all important thoroughfares ; the proposed alterations in these will tend to improve greatly the condition and appearance of other streets and thoroughfares contiguous to them. Castle-street, Wain-gate, and Castle-folds, formerly macadamised, and Barkers'-pool, Division-street and York-street, as well as other streets of less importance, and which were formerly set with boulders, have, within the last three years, been paved with square stones, and the foot-paths have also been widened, adding very much to the improved appearance of the sur-face, and enhancing the value of the property in the immediate vicinity.

It will be seen, on reference to Table I., that the public roads in this, as well as in the other districts, are, almost without exception, in a good state of repair.

The *North District* contains a greater extent of roads repaired by the town, public and private sewers, and a larger population than any other district. Of the 34 private roads more than 20 are in a state most disgraceful to the owners. Many might be named, bearing out this censure in the

* Now accomplished.

vicinity of Allen-street, as part of Morpeth-street, Ellis-street, Kenyon-street, Masdin-lane, Jericho, and Leicester-street. Several cases of fever have occurred in the last-mentioned street, unquestionably caused by the accumulation of filth and stagnant water, though in a situation which opens to the pure air of Crookes-moor, and which, from the naturally inclined position of this part of the town, might be effectually drained.*

Among the private roads- classed as " good," it would be an injustice to omit particular mention of two, formed by the governors of the Infirmary, which are set out with curb stones, and have large and efficient sewers Dixon-street has also been well set out and flagged, at a great expense, and is provided with a capacious sewer.

In this district, the boulder-pitched roads form a much larger proportion than in any other, there being fewer of a *first-rate* description, either as to respectability, or the amount of traffic upon them. There is in fact only one line of road from Snig-hill, along Westbar, Gibraltar-street and Shales moor to Philadelphia, that can be said to be of great importance. The traffic upon it is indeed greater than on any other in the town, excepting the line of road in the Park which has already been noticed. The cost of maintaining the Penistone road, *macadamised,* from Green-lane to Philadelphia, is consequently very heavy in proportion to its length. The average of the last four years has been £143 10s. 8d., and the length is only 308 yards.

The public sewers in this district are more extensive than in any other, and the capacity of some of them is also

* The Poor-Law Guardians are now partially removing the nuisance.

greater.   One line of sewers proceeds through five streets,
and is five feet high by four feet wide within.   Another,
passing through the same number of streets, is three feet six
inches high, and two feet six inches wide.   The old sewer
in Westbar-green, which, in consequence of its insufficiency,
for many years was a source of constant complaint and
annoyance, has recently been replaced by one extending
from the bottom of Silver-street head, along Westbar-green,
across the site of the Old Workhouse, down Workhouse-
lane into Love street, where it joins the large sewer above
mentioned.   It is five feet high and three feet wide within,
being three times the capacity of the old sewer.   The
deepest cutting in the construction of it was 16 feet, and
the total cost about £250.

From the general remarks made in the beginning of this
report, and from the cursory description of each district, in
explanation of the tables, the present condition of the roads
and sewers can scarcely fail to be well understood.   There
are matters of some importance connected with the economy
of road-making, which it is desirable to mention.   The
first is as to the comparative cost of macadamised and paved
roads ; they have already been compared upon a small scale,
in describing the Park district, where it was shown that
the cost per mile of the Park road is, per annum, £810
18s. 9¾d. ; while that of Duke-street, paved with boulders,
amounts only to £149 5s. 1½d.   And in speaking of the
North district, it was shown that the Penistone-road, from
Green-lane to Philadelphia, costs annually about 1s. per
superficial yard.   Now square stone paving, at 4s. per yard,
would last, in this case, at least eight years, and the even-
tual saving would be 50 per cent.

TABLE IV.

The following Table shews the total expenditure, and the quantity of material of various descriptions used; and of repairs in paving done for seven years in the Township of Sheffield, with the average per year.

Years.	Number of Roads Repaired	Flags.			Square Stones.			Boulders.			Curb Stones.			Common Sewers.			Ganister.	Limestone.	Furnace Cinders.	Salaries, Office and other expenses.			Gross Total Expenditure.		
		Yrds.	ft.	in.	Yrds.	ft.	in.	Yrds.	ft.	in.	Yrds.	ft.	in.	Yrds.	ft.	in.	Tons.	Tons.	Tons.	£.	s.	d.	£.	s.	d.
1834–5	117	13831	7	10	14874	1	3	26702	1	2	8056	0	6	750	1	6	4584⅓	1697½	545	900	15	10	9237	1	2
1836–7	180	14399	0	0	18890	4	6	30729	2	3	4271	0	0	467	0	0	2417	2788½	—	722	13	0⅓	8913	9	6½
1837–8	195	7866	2	4	18978	6	9	21576	0	0	2273	2	6	134	0	0	2545⅓	2639¾	—	887	19	6	8032	5	0½
1838–9	213	7377	6	9	18428	0	0	32990	3	8	2327	1	6	702	1	0	2312	2950¼	610¾	610	9	10⅓	8561	15	3½
1839-40	204	5134	1	6	17488	4	6	27698	8	0	1062	1	6	321	0	0	2737⅓	3360⅓	403	751	19	2½	8252	4	2
1840–1	202	8539	0	3	13884	5	10	26652	8	8	2079	0	9	335	0	0	2018¾	1926¼	152¼	971	11	6	7906	1	0½
1841–2	197	6997	0	0	10763	6	9	23805	0	0	3354	0	0	634	1	6	2359	2413¾	—	967	8	3	7534	7	7
Averag.	186 6/7	9163	5	3	16186	8	1	27164	8	6½	3346	0	11½	477	2	3½	2710 12 0	2539 10 0	244 8 2	830	8	2	8348	3	5

From the particulars given in this table, the annual cost of all the public macadamised carriage roads in the township may be deduced, and compared with the expense of all the other public roads and common sewers, made, enlarged, or repaired. It must also be borne in mind, that under the head of square stones is included the cost of 6,500 yards, the annual average of new paving, where the roads were formerly macadamised.

TABLE V.

Roads.	Average extent of 7 Years.	Description of Materials.	Quantity of Materials.	Cost of Repairs.	Expense per Mile per Annum.
			tons. cwt. qr.	£. s. d.	£. s. d.
Macdmsd.	7¼ miles.	Ganister,	2710 12 0	*	
		Limestone	2539 10 0	} 2197 16 2¼	303 2 11¼
		F. Cinders	244 8 2		
			Yds. ft. in.		
Paved,&c.	22¼ miles	Flags......	9163 5 3		
		Sqr.Stones	16186 8 1		
		Curb ditto	3346 0 11½	} 5319 19 0¼	236 8 10¼
		Boulders..	27164 8 6¼		
		Com.Sewr.	477 2 3½		

As already stated, the Surveyors of Highways had, until the year 1836, the power to repair, on the part of the town, such private roads as were deemed of sufficient importance,

* From the total average expenditure in Table IV., must be taken £830 8s. 2d. for salaries, office and other expenses, which leave £7517 15s. 3d. The price of material for macadamised roads at the various places where it is deposited, is 5s. 4½d. per ton, the breaking 1s. 1½d.; the weighing, piling, cartage, and laying on, 1s. 6d.; in the whole, 8s. per ton; or, £2197 16s. 2¼d. the total expense, which being deducted from the above sum, leaves £5319 19s. 0¼d. for the repair of all other kinds of roads and for Sewerage.

and a portion of the public funds was consequently expended in the making and repairing of them, which is now annually devoted to the extension of the square stone and boulder pavements, and to the improvement and more thorough repair of the public roads generally.

The effect of the town ceasing to make new roads, may be seen, on reference to Table IV., in the greatly decreased quantity of flags and curb-stones used annually, the flags used now being about half the quantity required in 1834-5, and the curb-stones only one-third ; as well in the increase, until the last two years, in the article of square-stones, nearly all the principal thoroughfares being now paved with that material. The total number of roads repaired per year has also greatly augmented, and yet the expenditure is less by nearly £2,000. The square stone pavement is now become very extensive, so that a person may travel through the town, from North to South, without passing over any other kind of road. An expeditious and economical mode of repairing the constant wear of these stones became, therefore, a great desideratum, and which, we are happy to say, has been most efficiently accomplished by the enterprising Surveyor, Mr. Lee, and the plan suggested by him is now in full operation. Men are employed who, in a standing position, with their faces covered with wire masks, cut down the elevated points of the road with a tool in the form of a hammer, containing a loose chisel, which is readily taken out and sharpened, and, in this manner, the surface is made more equal than any new pavement. It was used by way of trial in the streets for six months, and then, by order of the Board, a report was made to them, of which the following statement and table is a copy :—

"In this Report, only such parts of the streets as were
"in bad repair, have been taken into account, and while
"the payments to the men have been taken at rather more
"than the actual sums, the expense that would have been
"incurred in the ordinary repair of such streets would have
"been more than is stated in the report; for if labour, and
"lime, and sand, for re-setting, had been included at 1½d.
"per yard, it would have added a further sum of £58 12s.
"3d. to the saving by chipping, with three men for six
"months.   It may be observed that the whole of the streets
"did not require *immediately and entirely* repairing; but
"it must also be borne in mind that their condition would
"soon have been such as to make an entire repair neces-
"sary;—that the greater part was already in such a state;
"that a considerable proportion of new material would
"have been required; and that the longer the streets had
"remained unrepaired, the greater would have been that
"proportion.   This method of repairing streets, paved with
"square stones, has these further advantages over the old
"method of taking up, dressing and re-setting—that the
"stones are not loosened, and the foundation of the road
"not being disturbed, the progress of the work is not
"hindered by the most severe frost; the men have not to
"handle the stones, and therefore they can work as well
"in rainy weather as in dry;—and lastly, there is no stop-
"page of the road, during repairs, and when the men take
"away their tools at night, the road is free from any
"obstruction."

TABLE VI.

REPORT RESPECTING THE CHIPPING OF SQUARE STONE PAVING, TO FEBRUARY 27TH, 1840.

	COST OF CHIPPING					Expense of Taking up, Dressing, and Re-setting.		TOTAL AMOUNT SAVED.
	Men.		Cost of each Street.	Superficial Content.	Average per yard.	Price per Yard.	Cost of each Street.	
	Days.	Price.	£. s. d.	YARDS.	D.	s. D.	£. s. D.	£. s. D
Workhouse Croft..	7½ 1½	s. d. 2 10 4 6	1 6 2	240	1½	1 3	15 0 0	13 13 10
Westbar...........	78 15	2 10 4 6	13 14 4	2143	1½	1 3	133 18 9	120 4 5
Shales Moor	72½ 18	2 10 4 6	13 3 11	25779¾	1¼	1 3	161 1 8	147 17 9
Gibraltar-street...	70 14	2 10 4 6	14 6 10	1400	2¼	1 3	87 10 0	73 3 2
Haymarket........	120 42	2 10 4 6	26 9 0	2000	8¼	1 8	125 0 0	98 11 0
Fruit Market......	84 17	2 10 4 6	15 14 6	1018¼	3¼	1 3	63 12 11	47 18 5
Total......	Three men and tools 6 months		84 14 9	9878¾	2¾	1 3	586 3 4	501 8 7

It will be seen by this Table, that a portion of the labour
was performed by men who received 4s. 6d. per day, and
at the commencement of the undertaking, they were assisted
by a mason, who is no longer necessary; the whole work
is done now by labourers properly trained and superin-
tended.   A considerable variation in the average cost per
yard will be perceived, and this was caused by the stone in
some streets being much harder than that in others.

The following Table exhibits the further operations of
this plan, and the results are equally satisfactory.

TABLE VII.

STREET.	COST OF CHIPPING.				Average per Yd.	Expense of taking up, dressing, & re-setting the same.		Total Amount saved by Chippng
	Labourers.		Cost of each Street.	Supfl. Contnt		⅌ Yd.	Cost of each Street	
	Days.	Price.						

COMPARATIVE COST OF CHIPPING, FROM FEB. 27 TO SEPT. 27, 1840.

STREET.	Days.	Price (s.)	Cost of each Street (£ s. D.)	Supfl. Contnt (Yards.)	Average per Yd. (D.)	⅌ Yd. (s. D.)	Cost of each Street (£ s. D.)	Total Amount saved by Chippng (£ s. D.)
Market-street	55	3	8 5 0	498	4	1 3	31 2 6	22 17 6
Broad-street.........	45	3	6 15 0	1035	1¼	1 3	69 13 9	62 18 9
High-street	204½	3	30 12 9	1995	3¾	1 3	124 13 9	94 1 0
Bridge-street	116	3	17 8 0	1366	3	1 3	85 10 0	68 2 0
Church-street	149	3	22 7 0	1629	3½	1 3	101 16 3	79 9 3
Total	3 men&tools 7 months.		85 7 9	6525	3½	1 3	412 16 3	327 8 6

There are few places so favourably situated as this town
for obtaining materials for road.   It is surrounded by
quarries, furnishing flags, curb stones, ganister and square
paving stones.   The three first are of most excellent quality.
The square stone is a hard, compact, grey or brown quartz
sand-stone, immeasureably inferior to granite, but capable,
if well selected, of standing the traffic of almost any street
in the town at least eight years.   The limestone is brought
from a greater distance than any of the other material, being
carted from Eyam, Stoney Middleton, and Castleton, a
distance of twelve miles.

Little has been stated in this report respecting the public footpaths of the town. They are nearly all well-flagged, and are much wider than formerly. Broad curb stones began to be used about three years ago, and have very much improved the appearance of the footpaths generally. The extent of the public flagged footpaths in the township is about 47½ miles.

The extent and value of the materials of various descriptions upon the public roads, is a subject of interesting consideration, and, at some future period, may furnish data by which to ascertain the progressive improvement and extension of this description of public property, as well as to exhibit the increased accommodation and convenience to the inhabitants of Sheffield.

The public *flagged* footpaths would cover an area of 126,000 superficial yards,—the square stone pavement 92,785 yards,—the boulders of 162,360 yards, and the macadamized roads an area of 96,272 yards. The curbstones extend 90,000 yards, lineal measure ; the common sewers 18,397½ yards ; the grate soughs about 5,000 yards. The streets of the town contain 907 grates. The aggregate value of the roads is not less than £65,000.

In conclusion, the few roads described as "bad," in explanation of Table I., are of so little extent and importance as scarcely to affect the assertion, that the whole of the public roads in the township of Sheffield are in good condition, and the sewerage generally equal to the wants of a large and growing population.

There is perhaps no other large manufacturing town in the kingdom exhibiting so large a relative proportion of

streets in a good condition, both as respects the surface
and the sewerage. The number of public and private
roads is 387 ; and 13 public roads only can with justice
be called *bad*, and 78 private; total 91. In Leeds, the
number of streets is 586, and the *bad* and *very bad* are
233, which is a much greater proportion. The public
roads wholly sewered in this town are 83 ; partly so, 44 ;
total, 127. The private roads, wholly and partially sewered,
26 ; total, public and private, 153 ; nearly one-half of the
existing roads. In Leeds, the public roads wholly sewered,
38 ; private, 3 ; total, 40 : public and private roads partly
sewered, 47 ; total, 87. The roads not sewered and not
ascertained, amount to the number of 499. The present
excellent condition of the streets of this town is to be
ascribed principally to two causes,—a better system of
management, and an intelligent and enterprising Surveyor.
On the old system, which continued till within a few years,
four gentlemen were elected annually to the office of Surveyors, and in the majority of cases, their fitness for the
duties was no consideration with the public by whom they
were elected. Great interest was usually made by gentlemen solicitous for the office, for the purpose of enhancing
the value of their own property, by improving the condition
of the roads in its immediate vicinity. In all such efforts
they readily secured the aid of their neighbours. According
to such a system of mismanagement, it was scarcely
reasonable to expect anything but partial improvements.
It often happened that streets, comparatively private, or
little used, had an amount of money expended upon them
that would have efficiently repaired half a dozen public
roads. The grossness of the evil at last led to its correction.
A permanent Surveyor was appointed, practically acquainted
with road-making, who is allowed to have the entire

direction and superintendence of the business.   It has been his study to form an efficient system of sewerage, and . he has for years been carrying out a well-digested plan, that will ultimately render this town, in all probability, inferior to none in the kingdom, in regard to the drainage and superficial condition of the streets.   The present surveyor* is a gentleman of considerable scientific attainments, and by his intelligence, skill, and devotion to the practical duties of his office, has conferred incalculable benefits upon the town, not only in important improvements which he suggests and carries out, but in the immense saving of expenditure.   We regret that his sphere of usefulness is confined to *one* town.   The character of his mind and acquirements fits him for a far more extensive field of utility.

* Mr. William Lee.

CHAPTER VII.

COMPARISON OF THE RELATIVE EXPENCES OF THE HIGHWAYS IN THE TOWNSHIPS OF SHEFFIELD, ECCLESALL BIERLOW, AND BRIGHTSIDE BIERLOW.

We beg to direct attention to the following particulars respecting the length and condition of roads, and expences of repair in each of the above townships. They are worthy of consideration. They show the advantages of scientific management, and the evils arising from the want of it. The township of Sheffield, in the department of the highways, has an excellent staff of permanently paid officers, with the exception of Brightside Bierlow; while the other townships, have been principally in the hands of contractors and jobbers, without vigilant superintendence, or any comprehensive plan of procedure. The tables exhibit a remarkable difference in the character of the results. Table VIII. gives the lengths of the several kinds of road and of common sewers in the township of Sheffield, in Ecclesall Bierlow and Brightside Bierlow. No official estimate, under either head, has been given by the two latter townships, nor do they possess the facts necessary to the calculation. The statements in both cases are the result of personal investigation, and may be regarded as a close approximation to the truth.

TABLE VIII.

TOWNSHIP.	EXTENT OF THE VARIOUS KINDS OF PUBLIC CARRIAGE ROADS.			Total extnt of Public Carriage Roads.	Extent of Public Sewerage.	Population 1841
	Square Stones.	Boulders.	Macdmised			
	M. F. P.	M. F. P.	M. F. P.	M. F. P.	M. F. P.	
Sheffield	7 4 10	15 3 14	6 6 15	29 5 39	10 3 25	69,587
Ecclesall Bierlow	0 3 24	3 3 18	28 0 38	32 0 0	1 3 16	19,964
Brightsd. Bierlow	0 0 17	0 0 32	19 1 26	19 2 35	0 3 4	10,089

From this table, it is evident that about four-fifths of all the public roads in the township of Sheffield are *paved ;* in Ecclesall less than one-eighth, and in Brightside about $\frac{1}{15}$. The common sewers in Sheffield extend under more than one-third *in length* of the roads ; in Ecclesall Bierlow, the proportion is $\frac{1}{12}$, and in Brightside Bierlow $\frac{1}{50}$.

A general idea of the wear of public roads may be formed from the population of the respective townships,—from the sums expended in the repair of turnpike and other principal roads in the vicinity of the town, and also from the amount arising from tolls. Several of the most important carriage roads in Ecclesall and Brightside are kept in condition by turnpike trustees, while in Sheffield all the public roads are maintained by the township alone ; and eight years ago, when a great extension of the pavements took place, the roads generally were much worse than at present, indeed since that period they have exhibited a constantly improving condition. Table I. shews that a great part of the town, as was formerly the case, has not been neglected in order that money might be lavishly expended in particular situations, to gratify private individuals. Tables IX., X., and XI. present, at one view, the annual disbursements under several heads, and the expenditure in each of the three townships.

H

98

TABLE IX

TOWNSHIP OF SHEFFIELD.

Year.	Paid for stone and leading for macadamised roads.			Stone breaking and labour.			Boulder pitching.			Masons, for paving.			Curb stones, plodders, and channelling.			Flags.			Square stones.			Common sewers.			Amount in the Pound levied.		Total expenditure.		
	£	s.	D.	£	s.	D.	£	s.	D.	£	s.	D.	£	s.	D.	£	s.	D.	£	s.	D.	£	s.	D.	s.	D.	£	s.	D.
1884-5	1650	11	8	973	8	10	784	11	4	1314	15	1	388	5	5	902	17	5	1187	12	5	542	16	0	3	0	9237	1	2
1886-7	1461	11	5	1078	1	7	798	8	7	1870	15	6	268	10	11	962	13	0	697	13	6	181	12	0	1	6	8913	9	6¼
1887-8	1477	15	8¼	1145	1	4¼	585	5	8	1457	19	5	143	19	5	505	19	6	1098	7	4	39	18	4	1	4	8082	5	0¼
1888-9	1614	5	0	1193	13	10	874	19	4	1377	15	11	193	12	11	1488	13	11	1004	18	11	305	11	11	1	4	8561	15	3½
1889-40	1863	10	6	1301	3	6	689	6	10	1327	17	7	86	7	6	286	8	6	1229	18	6	213	16	10	1	4	8252	4	2
1840-1	1243	9	9½	1288	18	0	614	15	2	1254	17	4	248	16	5	422	13	6	780	4	11	249	10	11	0	8	7906	1	0½
1841-2	1435	1	1	1224	18	7	503	12	7	1027	10	11	244	2	2	422	13	2	599	2	9	349	18	8	1	2	7534	7	7

TABLE X.

TOWNSHIP OF ECCLESALL BIERLOW.

Year.	Paid for stone and leading for macadamised roads.			Stone breaking and labour.			Boulder pitching.			Masons, for paving.			Curb stones, boulders, and channeling.			Flags.			Square stones.			Amount in the Pound levied.		Total expenditure.		
	£	s.	D.	£	s.	D.	£	s	D.	£	s.	D.	£	s.	D.	£	s.	D.	£	s.	D.	s.	D.	£	s.	D.
1834-5	238	13	1	478	6	1½	110	13	5	298	0	3½	71	17	11	395	16	0	91	2	1	3	0	2103	13	4
1836-7	263	4	4½	850	5	6	265	7	8	Inclusive.			----			673	10	10	Inclusive.			1	5½	3048	0	6½
1837-8	615	11	5	477	14	3	190	9	0	Do.			73	4	9	253	10	7	Do.			0	5	2354	2	0
1838-9	656	18	9	1020	1	10½	299	5	0	Do.			----			539	0	1	474	1	1	2	1	3547	4	7½
1839-40	1249	16	7	1525	18	3	338	15	8	Do.			----			441	9	2	216	2	0	2	1	4210	0	7
1840-1	569	18	0	731	0	8	176	12	0	Do.			----			1076	14	10	127	5	0	1	8	3860	14	8
1841-2	1001	13	11	456	16	3½	----			1414	4	2	Inclusive			----			797	11	6	1	8	4361	8	10

H 2

TABLE XI.

Township of Brightside Bierlow.

Year.	Paid for stone and leading for macadamised roads.	Stone breaking and labour.	Boulder pitching.	Masons, for paving.	Curb stones, plodders, & channelling	Flags.	Square stones.	Amount in the Pound levied.	Total expenditure.
	£ s. D.	£ s. D.	£ s. D.	£ s. D.	£ s. D.	£ s. D.	£ s. D.	s. D.	£ s. D.
1834-5	Unknown.	Unknown.	Unknown.	Unknown.	Unknwn.	Unknown.	Unknown.	Unkn.	Unknown.
1836 7	306 5 8½	376 9 2½	0 15 8	11 3 11½	26 15 10	0 0 0	0 0 0	2 6	1071 12 6½
1837-8	359 14 4	455 2 8	0 0 0	24 2 5	6 3 2	3 2 0	1 16 0	1 8	1053 11 1
1838-9	514 6 6	451 18 2½	0 0 0	91 5 10	11 12 7	43 2 0	14 0 4½	2 6	1300 5 0½
1839-40	441 3 10½	411 5 3	9 0 0	107 7 6	63 7 6	76 0 9	16 11 2	2 6	1431 12 5½
1840-1	476 4 7	366 14 0½	7 10 6	67 0 1	38 9 10	81 7 8	42 12 10	*1 0	1318 10 7½
1841-2	442 17 8	331 5 0	1 11 0	100 16 2	14 18 9	44 8 2	39 5 0	1 0	1314 2 4½

* A new valuation of the township was made in that year.

According to these tables, it appears that during the last seven years, while considerable improvements have been in progress in the township of Sheffield, necessarily demanding a large outlay of capital, the total expenditure has gradually *decreased* to the extent of TWENTY per cent.   In Ecclesall Bierlow it has gradually *increased* during, the same period, *one hundred per cent.*   In Brightside Bierlow, within the last *six* years, (no accounts before that time are accessible) the increase has been *twenty per cent.*   It would occupy much time and space to enter upon the consideration of the causes of these striking differences.   The facts presented would lead us to infer that the management in Brightside Bierlow is much superior to that in Ecclesall Bierlow. The sums paid for flags and square stones by the different townships, as far as can be ascertained from the irregular manner in which the accounts of Ecclesall Bierlow are kept, explain one part of the anomaly.   Tables IX. and X. shew, that during this period, the amount expended by Ecclesall in flags has doubled, while that of Sheffield has been reduced one half, and that now the expenses under this head are about equal in the two townships.   The fluctuating character of the sums paid, under each of the several heads in Table X, exhibits, we are afraid, the absence of any scientific management.

In analyzing these tables, it must be recollected, that while flagged causeways or paved carriage roads may last some years, without requiring any repair, macadamized roads demand an *annual* outlay, and which varies little in amount during a period of ten years, as may be seen in the first two columns in Tables IX. and XI.   The corresponding columns in Table X. shew, that the macadamized roads in Ecclesall cost in 1839-40, £2,775 14s. 10d.,

when, five years previously they had been maintained for
£716 19s. 2½d.   It may perhaps be asked how, in 1840-1,
the amount was reduced to £1300. 18s. 8d. ; the answer
will be found in the sum £1076. 14s. 10d. expended that
year in flags.   In Tables IX. and XI. the expense of stone
breaking and accompanying labour, is generally somewhat
less than the value of the material.   In Table X. the cost
of labour is mostly *greater*, and its variations range in
the following order :—½, ⅝, ⅓, ¼, ⅙, ⅚, and last year the
proportion was less than ⅓.   Similar irregularities exist
under other heads in this Table.   They are less evident
from the confused manner in which the particulars are
sometimes entered.

In Table IX., the sums under the head common sewers
vary considerably, which is occasioned by the making of
new sewers in different years.   In the same table, the square
stones purchased in 1840-1, and in 1841-2, were much
less than for several preceding years; this is principally
owing to the method of chipping the surface of the square
stone pavements, already alluded to at some length, and
which was brought into operation in the latter part of the
year 1839.

CHAPTER VIII.

PHYSICAL CONDITION OF THE POPULATION.

ANALYTICAL TABLE OF BIRTHS AND DEATHS IN THE SHEFFIELD REGISTRATION DISTRICT, ARRANGED IN YEARS FROM JULY 1ST, 1837, TO JUNE 30TH, 1842.

	1837-8	1838-9	1839-40	1840-1	1841-2	Total five Years.
Under 1	556	608	638	635	546	2983
1	282	357	272	274	326	1511
2 to 4	243	343	403	262	293	1544
5 to 9	104	127	216	113	112	672
10 to 19	107	120	145	141	129	642
20 to 29	158	193	171	163	131	716
30 to 39	164	135	164	148	145	756
40 to 49	143	142	137	167	120	709
50 to 59	136	142	156	145	142	721
60 to 69	150	133	165	158	138	744
70 to 79	112	110	100	140	139	601
80 to 89	46	40	49	43	48	226
90 to 99	7	4	4	3	10	24
Total deaths	2,208	2,450	2,610	2,392	2,284	11,944
Total births	3,261	3,617	3,652	3,523	3,451	17,504

The proportion of the deaths of infants varies greatly in different parts of the kingdom. In the foregoing table, the deaths under one year have been 250 out of 1000 deaths at all ages. In the mining parts of Staffordshire, in Leeds and its suburbs, the deaths under one year have been 270 out of 1000 deaths at all ages; while in some of the Northern parts of England, the proportion has been about 180.* Similar differences are also observed in the proportion of deaths under five years of age, as is shown by the following table:—

Deaths of Children under five years of age, and of the aged above 70, out of 1000 deaths at all ages, in the subjoined places or districts.

	Under 5.	Above 70.
Manchester and Salford (Registration District)...	517	58
Sheffield (Registration District)	506	71
Leeds (Registration District)	504	74
Liverpool and West Derby	480	63
Birmingham	453	80
Metropolis	401	103
England and Wales	393	143
Yorkshire (Northern part) and Durham............	322	206

The deaths under five years exhibit smaller proportions with respect to the dense populations, than would be observed were not the deaths at other ages proportionally enlarged by immigration of older persons from the agricultural districts. The same circumstances will, in a minor degree, affect the deaths above seventy.

The following table gives the deaths, at the several seasons of one year, in this and other towns on which we shall make a few remarks, exposing the sources of fallacy in such returns, from which are deduced the general rate of mortality for the respective towns:—

* First Annual Report of the Registrar General, page 15, 1839.

DEATHS IN THE FOUR QUARTERS OF 1842, IN THE
FOLLOWING TOWNS.

	Population in 1841.	Winter.	Spring.	Summer	Autumn.	Averg. deaths in four annual quarters. 1838 1841	Total of four seasons.	Reciprocal of Mortality.
Sheffield	85,076	740	485	501	456	674	2182	39.0
Huddersfield	107,140	561	547	444	444	516	1996	55.6
Halifax	109,175	614	549	488	621	545	2262	48.3
Bradford	132,164	885	835	820	783	789	3323	39.8
Leeds	168,667	1335	1165	1133	982	1159	4613	36.5
Hull	41,130	244	"271	270	257	326	1042	45.9
York	47.779	313	314	255	251	265	1133	42.2
Total....	691,131	4692	4166	3911	3794	4274	16563	41.7

The comparison which is here given of the rate of
mortality is altogether unjust and irregular: these districts
are compounded, very unequally, of town and village
populations; thus of 85,000 in the Sheffield district, about
75,000 may be of an oppidan character, in which the
reciprocal index of mortality is perhaps about thirty-three,
if not less, whilst the rural portion may die at the rate of
one in forty-five or fifty, according to locality. In Huddersfield, as an illustration of these remarks, the great
majority live in manufacturing villages and rural districts,
hence the evidence of a very low rate of mortality, and
the same may be said of Halifax and, to a great extent,
of Leeds.

The probable inference is, that town populations have a
rate of mortality, varying in the complicate ratio of magnitude and density, in some degree affected by locality.   In
villages of rural character, the mortality is of the lightest
description; whilst the suburban districts of large towns
partake of both characters, and the mortality is proportionately modified.

The proper data will be—the registered deaths for
several years,—the mean populations respectively for the

middle of the intervals of registry, or sufficient collateral data for inferring these particulars, and a very minute distinction of the classes of the inhabitants

Attention to these circumstances, calculating also the rate of mortality on the proportions of the population, which are purely oppidan, suburban and rural, separately, which in the above and all similar returns, are mixed together, can alone present accurate results. The calculations on the general returns, convey a very imperfect idea of the rate of mortality among the labouring classes, hence of their suffering, struggling and wretchedness. Were such an estimate made at the present time, in relation to them, according to these distinctions, on the deaths in this town and in several of the manufacturing places mentioned, it would be appalling to contemplate. As an illustration of the necessity of such distinctions, we shall shortly present a table of the rate of mortality, at different ages, in a registration district, the population of which though, to a considerable extent, oppidan, is yet largely suburban and rural in its character.

The difference, in the degree in which the various classes of the population are. mixed together, in the registration returns of the several towns, to which we have alluded, is to be traced chiefly to the nature of the trade carried on. The staple manufactures of this town cannot conveniently be conducted, on an extensive scale, in the neighbouring villages. Many of the articles produced undergo numerous processes, and demand a proportionate variety of hands possessing different kinds of skill, which, with few exceptions, co-exist only in the town. Indeed the materials of the articles being metal, the conveyance of them to and from the country would be a serious disadvantage to any manufacturer. Several of the processes are carried on in the villages by small masters and artisans, such as the forging of forks, table-blades, and the cutting of files.

The manufactures peculiar to Huddersfield, Halifax, Bradford and Leeds, find employment for thousands in the neighbouring rural districts. In these, large mills frequently abound, and, the workmen engaged in them have the advantage of country habitations, which modify materially the rate of mortality compared with a town population. Independently, however, of these extensive establishments, immense numbers are employed in their own dwellings or in small workshops, consequently are unaffected by various causes, which in densely crowded districts, embitter and abbreviate human existence. These remarks are sufficient to shew, how necessary it is, in stating the rate of mortality on the registration returns of the population of any town, to point out the circumstances of the individuals incorporated in them.

CAUSES OF DEATH IN THE SHEFFIELD REGISTRATION DISTRICT.

	1837-8	1838-9	1839-40	1840-1	1841-2	Total of 5 years
Accidents (returned by Coroner)	112	113	155	144	94	618
Apoplexy	20	17	23	22	11	87
Asthma	40	37	56	40	33	206
Abscess	0	0	2	8	10	20
Bloody flux	0	0	0	0	1	1
Consumption	435	390	362	237	210	1604
Convulsions	193	134	213	205	174	919
Cramp at stomach	0	0	0	0	1	1
Croup	0	47	42	32	45	166
Childbirth	0	20	31	13	0	64

	1837-8	1838-9	1839-40	1840-1	1841-2	Total of 5 years
Cancer	0	0	2	12	12	26
Cholera	0	0	0	2	2	4
Disease of the Bladder ...	0	0	2	0	0	2
───────── Legs	0	0	0	2	0	2
───────── Liver	0	29	22	25	30	106
───────── Head	0	0	0	19	18	37
───────── Heart......	0	16	21	26	22	85
───────── Spine	0	0	4	10	3	17
───────── Womb ...	0	0	1	1	0	2
Debility	0	118	223	78	100	519
Decay of Nature	138	126	148	195	193	800
Decline	0	0	0	219	127	346
Dentition	83	84	108	68	83	426
Dementia	0	0	0	0	1	1
Dropsy	0	0	0	0	51	51
─────── of the Chest	0	0	0	0	22	22
─────── of the Head	0	0	0	0	59	59
Delirium tremens	0	0	2	0	1	3
Diabetes......................	0	0	2	1	3	6
Dysentry......................	0	0	0	1	1	2
Epilepsy......................	0	0	0	1	3	4
Erysipelas	0	0	7	3	9	19
Fever, Common.............	150	27	43	19	16	255
─────── Bilious	0	0	0	0	3	3
─────── Brain............	0	0	0	4	31	35
─────── in the Head	0	0	0	5	0	5
─────── Worm	0	0	0	0	3	3
─────── Milk	0	0	0	0	1	1
─────── Rheumatic	0	0	3	3	2	8
─────── Scarlet	0	61	448	30	11	550
─────── Typhus	0	0	0	0	0	30*
Fits.............................	0	0	0	0	1	1
Fistula	0	0	0	1	1	2
Gravel.........................	0	0	0	0	4	4
Hernia	0	0	1	1	0	2
Hooping Cough.............	0	160	23	75	29	287
Hemorrhage	0	0	0	1	2	3
Inflammations not distinguished	280	0	0	0	0	280
Inflammation of Bladder,	0	0	0	3	0	3
──────────── Bowels ...	0	115	80	109	93	397

* The cases for each year are not given.

	1837-8	1838-9	1839-40	1840-1	1841-2	Total of 5 years
———— Brain......	0	119	97	80	55	351
———— Lungs ...	0	247	216	195	216	874
———— Windpipe	0	0	2	0	5	7
Jaundice..........	0	11	4	5	8	28
Influenza	0	0	0	4	1	5
Leprosy	0	0	0	1	0	1
Locked Jaw	0	0	1	1	0	2
Marasmus	0	0	0	1	0	1
Measles	169	112	10	7	32	330
Miscarriage	0	0	0	0	2	2
Mortification	0	0	0	1	2	3
Old Age	0	0	0	0	9	9
Paralysis...................	0	28	17	26	36	107
Pleurisy	0	0	4	7	1	12
Premature Birth	0	0	11	16	31	58
Rupture of Blood Vessel,	0	0	0	1	2	3
Scrofula	0	0	1	1	0	2
Small Pox	93	46	10	161	5	315
Thrush	0	0	4	7	1	12
Tumour	0	0	3	3	1	7
Ulcers	0	0	1	4	0	5
Venereal complaint	0	0	0	0	1	1
Various diseases not particularly specified ... }	350	137	31	23	26	567
Want of Food	0	0	0	0	1	1
	2208	2450	2610	2392	2283	11954

Table shewing in 100(000) Deaths, the number of deaths from Phthisis :—

1837-38	19(701)
1838-39	15(918)
1839-40	13(870)
1840-41	19(064)
Mean of the four years	17(138)

This proportion of deaths is a little under the general average of the kingdom. This is stated to be about 20 per cent of the total number of deaths, or nearly four annually out of every 1000 living.* The proportion to the living in this town is here given, and compared with returns from other places.

Annual deaths to 100(000) living :—

Sheffield	.498
Leeds	.401
Birmingham	.494
Manchester	.510
London	.402
Liverpool	.670

Typhus fever seldom exists to any great extent in this district. It is indeed much less prevalent than in most other large manufacturing towns, as the following calculations show.

Deaths from typhus in 100(000) Deaths.)

Sheffield, mean of three years	1.551
Metropolis	7.855
Manchester and Salford	7.530
Liverpool and West Derby	10.833
Leeds	4.688
Birmingham	5.338
England and Wales	6.390

Some of the returns respecting the causes of death, we are afraid, are not much to be depended upon. There is by no means sufficient care exercised by many medical practitioners in the discrimination of the nature of fatal diseases. They are not duly impressed with the importance of accuracy in this matter. In the preceding table, we have

* First Report of the Registrar General, page 74, 1839.

returns under the head of consumption, decay of nature, decline and old age. Decline, in the ordinary acceptation of the term, is understood to be consumption, and decay of nature will certainly include the deaths from old age. We have no hesitation in asserting, that many who are stated to have died of asthma were cases of consumption. Several of the manufactures carried on in this town, produce to a great extent phthisis, the symptoms of which are frequently masked by those of asthma, by which is understood, difficulty of breathing, cough and expectoration, continuing for years, without any great attenuation of the body. Many of these cases might with greater propriety be designated consumption. One death is stated to arise from want of food. The observation of any medical practitioner must indeed be very limited, that has not led him to the conclusion, that the deaths of hundreds in this town are to be traced to a deficiency of the necessaries of life. They may die of disease, but this is induced by poor living, conjoined with laborious exertion. We speak from a personal and extensive knowledge of the condition of the working classes.

Were the legitimate cases of consumption, drawn from those recorded as asthma, decay of nature and decline, and added to those properly so designated, the proportion would greatly exceed what is stated. We do not think that the locality predisposes in a peculiar degree to phthisis, but, on the contrary, is healthy. The high mortality by which it is distinguished, arises from the nature of the manufactures carried on. Many of the branches are extremely destructive to human life, perhaps to a much greater extent than the staple manufactures of any town in the kingdom.

In order to ascertain the nature of the diseases prevailing among the working classes, at the present period of depression, and during the winter season, we procured from the books of the surgeons, at the poor-house, the names, ages, occupations and diseases of two hundred persons then, or immediately before, under medical treatment. They were not selected, but taken indiscriminately; hence, saving the modifying influence of the seasons, they will convey a generally correct idea of the diseases to which the labouring classes in this town are particularly subject. The analysis of the two hundred persons furnishes the following particulars :—

File cutters	13
File grinders	2
File hardeners	4
File forgers	7
Spring knife cutlers	53
Pen and pocket blade grinders	3
Table blade forgers	4
Table blade strikers.............................	2
Table blade grinders	25
Table knife cutlers	12
Razor smiths	4
Razor grinders....................................	6
Fork grinders	2
Silversmiths	4
White metalsmiths	2
Moulders	2
Fender makers....................................	2
Comb makers	3
Saw handle maker	1
Saw makers	5
Scale cutters and pressers	12
Scissorsmiths	4
Labourers...	8
Miscellaneous trades	23
	200

The ages of the Two hundred :—

From 20 to 25 58
—   26 to 30 39
—   31 to 35 21
—   36 to 40 26
—   41 to 45 15
—   46 to 50 12
—   51 to 55 20
—   61 to 65 5
—   66 to 70 3
        74 1

        200

The diseases with which they were affected, or under which they had laboured, may be classified as follows :—

I. Diseases of the air passages .... 60 cases.
II.   —   of the digestive apparatus ...... 25 —
III.   —   of the urinary organs .... 7 —
IV.   —   of the nervous system .... 19 —
V.   —   of the heart .... 3 —
VI.   —   of the skin........................... 3 —
VII. Diarrhœa and Dysentery..................... 26 —
VIII. Rheumatism .... 25 —
IX. Fever .... 10 —
X. Debility .... 3 —
XI. Miscellaneous .... 19 —

In class I. are included numerous cases of Bronchitis, Pleuritis, Asthma, Catarrh, and several cases of Phthisis. In class II. the various forms of Indigestion. In III., Dysuria, Hæmaturia and Gravel. In IV., different Neuralgic affections—Paralysis and Epilepsy. These four classes include one hundred and eleven cases of the two hundred. The preceding particulars suggest a few remarks of importance. It is often alleged by the manufacturers, that the artisans in the best paid branches are

I

the most dissipated, reckless and improvident, and their families in the least comfortable circumstances. The whole of our inquiries establish the contrary. The best paid are always the last to apply to the parish, and, in a protracted period of distress, a less proportion, according to their numbers, are always found recipients of charity. Among the foregoing trades, there are two, the pen and the table knife branches,* which are unquestionably the worst remunerated in the town, in all conditions of trade, especially the former, and the cases in these two branches are ninety-six of the two hundred, which is indeed an extraordinary proportion. Neither of them is in union, or protected by any form of combination.

The ages of the individuals receiving medical treatment would, in conjunction with other facts, indicate a high rate of mortality among the working classes. Of the two hundred cases, one hundred and eighteen are under thirty-five years of age. Such are the results furnished by an analysis of two hundred cases, taken indiscriminately from the books of the medical officers of the Poorhouse.

The chief causes of the high mortality are—1. The injurious tendency of the occupations. 2. The prevailing dissipation among great numbers of the working classes. 3. Early and improvident marriages. In regard to the first head, it is scarcely necessary to state, that in the grinding branches, in which some thousands of artisans are employed, a higher rate of mortality is the result, accompanied with a greater amount of suffering and wretchedness

* The table knife branch was in union until within the past twelve months, and expended nearly £20,000 in the endeavour to maintain it.

than is found in connexion with any manufactures in the kingdom. The baneful tendency of the trade is not confined to dry grinding; the position in which the artisans work is exceedingly unfavourable to the action of the lungs, the upper half of the body being constantly bent forward over the revolving stone; and in the branches in which dry grinding is not used, the articles, such as saws, scythes and edge tools, are heavy, demanding great muscular exertion. Independently, however, of the bodily exhaustion which is occasioned, the grinders are exceedingly subject to acute inflammatory diseases, from the exposed situations in which they work.

Dissipation has always existed to a painful extent among great numbers of the grinders, which is to be ascribed to several circumstances. In general they are put to work very early, without having received any education whatever, hence their ignorance is the source of many evils They have few mental resources of enjoyment within themselves. One prominent and most baneful evil springing out of this ignorance, is early marriages. The ability to support a wife, never appears to be a consideration with many of them, and indeed the more indigent they are, the earlier do they marry, and a large proportion of this class of grinders marry girls employed in manufactures, whose habits and ignorance of household affairs, are ill-calculated to enable them to use, to the best advantage, what is earned. We speak from extensive enquiries when we assert, that the more wretched the condition of the artisans and the earlier do they marry.

In our opinion, the employment of girls in shops is fraught with a greater amount of evil to the well-being

I 2

of society, than almost any other cause co-existent with
manufactures.   It is the source of a low tone of morality,
ignorance and suffering.   In some of the branches of trade
carried on in this town, girls are extensively employed, and
with few exceptions, in the same room with men and boys,
or pursue their labours in constant intercourse with them.
As long as this practice prevails, much of the good that
education would produce will be counteracted, and generation after generation will arise, presenting little improvement in feelings or habits.

Many of the manufactures of this town are detrimental
to health, from the severe bodily exertions which they
unceasingly demand, and the varying degrees of temperature to which the workmen are exposed.   There is one
circumstance which tends in an especial manner to produce
dissipation, and its inevitable result—a high rate of mortality,—viz. :   the independent position of an immense
number of the workmen.   Thousands of them do not work
on the premises of their employers, and, therefore, are under
no surveillance or control ;   and even when such is the case,
they too frequently begin and cease to labour according
to their own whim or pleasure.   To this peculiar circumstance, in the position of the workmen, may be traced much
of the prevailing dissipation in times of good trade.   In a
period of depression, as at present existing, the wages, in
many of the branches are miserably low ; hence the artisans,
to earn what is quite inadequate to the maintenance of their
families, are under the necessity of labouring hard, with
constitutions breaking up from exertion and insufficient
nourishment.

THE GENERAL RATIOS OF MORTALITY, IN DIFFERENT
YEARS, INFERRED FROM THE AMOUNTS OF POPULATION
CALCULATED, SEVERALLY, AT THE MIDDLE PERIODS
OF THOSE YEARS.

The registration year is from Midsummer to Midsummer,
by which the difficulty of calculation is increased, for we
are obliged to interpolate by half years, to ascertain the
probable population at the commencement of each year.

There is some little embarrassment in pursuing the
inquiry, the population of Handsworth, one of the outer
divisions, not being given in the census of 1831, along
with the remainder of the district. The difficulty being
surmounted by comparison, the population of the registration
district of the town, for the undermentioned periods, will be

1838	83,608
1839	84,653
1840	85,569
1841	86,353
1842	87,001

From these results, and the elements already given, we
deduce the following :—

	1837-8	1838-9	1839-40	1840-1	1841-2	Mean of 5 years.
Persons living to each birth	25.6	23.4	23.4	26.1	25.2	24.9
Persons living to each death	37.9	34.6	32.8	36.1	38.1	35.9

In making these comparisons, particular attention must
always be given to the population existing at the middle
point of the time, over which the births or deaths extend.
If the population cannot be accurately obtained, either
from direct or collateral data, for the whole period of registration, the calculations will only be an approximation to
the truth.

The census of 1841 was taken about the middle of the year :* the middle point of the two years of Registration, 1840-41 and 1841-2, occurring at the end of June, 1841, the births and deaths for the mean of these two years, will correspond so nearly with the date of the census, that there will be no difficulty in ascertaining what may be considered the present, or most recent rates of mortality in Sheffield, its sub-divisions, and in the outer divisions of the district.

Previous to this, however, the census of the subdivisions of the Township have to be enlarged about one in 42, to make the published census of the Superintendant Registrar agree with the returns from the Registrar General's office. Thus modified, the exact population of the sub-divisions of this township will become :—

Park	12,246
South	14,550
West	16,544
North	26,246
Township of Sheffield	69,587

The mean annual registered deaths for the two years in question will then be :—

Park	313¼
South	346¼
West	423¼
North	874
	2,335

These two statements being as nearly synchronous as the data will admit, we proceed, by their co-application, to deduce the following *general reciprocal* rates of mortality, the accuracy of which cannot be doubted, and they are interesting to contemplate, as evidence of the diversified rates of mortality in the town, according to the character and density of the population in each division of it.

* June 7th.

Annual Deaths :—

	One in
Park district	39.1
South district	42.0
West district....................................	39.1
North district	30.0
Township of Sheffield	35.5

The aggregate result stated for the township is not the numerical average of the four districts, which would be unjust, as the North district is immensely more populous than the others. Each item has been calculated on independent data.

The coincidence in value of the general rates of mortality in the Park and West districts, arises from the fact, that in these are found the two extreme classes of society, the labouring and indigent, and the comparatively independent and comfortable ; the former, however, largely prevails.

We now proceed to the consideration of the primary divisions of the Registration district ; the population for each is previously accurately given for the middle of 1841, and the mean annual deaths for the two years are as follows :—

Township of Sheffield	1,957½
Brightside Bierlow	229½
Attercliffe-cum-Darnall	97½
Handsworth	50½
Sheffield Registration district	2,335

By calculation, the general reciprocal rates of mortality are found to be :—

	One in
Township of Sheffield	35.5
Brightside Bierlow	44.0
Attercliffe-cum-Darnall	42 6
Handsworth	56.7
Sheffield Registration district...............	37.1

Here we observe a marked difference in the average
duration of life in the divisions of the Registration district.
In the township of Sheffield, one in 35.5 dies annually,
while in Handsworth, the population of which is chiefly
employed in agriculture, only one in 56.7. In a previous page
we have alluded to the Ecclesall Bierlow registration district,
part of which is in the parish of Sheffield, though not
included in the registration district of it, the population of
which, as already remarked, is partly oppidan, suburban
and rural. The rates of mortality are found to be in
harmony with the diversities in the character of the district.

COMPARATIVE SUMMARY MORTALITY, AT THE DIFFERENT
  AGES OF INFANCY AND ADVANCED LIFE, IN SHEFFIELD
  AND ITS RURAL VICINITIES.

Deaths under 5 and above 70 years of age, to each 1000
deaths at all ages, in the Sheffield registration district :—

Division.	Under 5.	Above 70.
Sheffield Township	513	67
Brightside Bierlow	463	101
Attercliffe-cum-Darnall.........	511	82
Handsworth	434	158
Total Registration District ...	506	71

In the Township of Sheffield :—

Subdivisions.	Under 5.	Above 70.
Park	574	64
South	482	73
West	522	64
North	495	68
Whole Township	513	67

Mean ages of individuals dying above given ages, in the Registration districts of Sheffield and Ecclesall Bierlow, in their divisions, and in the subdivisions of the Township of Sheffield.

Above the age of	Districts		Divisions of the Sheffield Registration District				Divisions of Ecclesall Bierlow Reg. District		Subdivisions of the Township of Sheffield.			
	Sheffield.	Ecclesall Bierlow.	Sheffield Township.	Brightside Bierlow.	Attercliffe-cum-Darnall.	Handsworth.†	Ecclesall Bierlow Township.	Remaind*.	Park.	South.	West.	North.
0	21.44	28.84	21.27	25.24	21.86	27.42	28.09	26.28	18.21	22.44	21.66	21.91
5	42.16	43.07	41.81	45.85	43.38	47.31	42.69	44.62	40.70	42.38	41.52	41.88
10	46.75	47.20	45.88	49.47	48.24	48.94	47.08	47.96	44.62	46.08	45.67	45.96
20	52.39	52.02	50.06	53.52	54.04	55.08	51.53	52.70	50.48	51.31	49.14	50.04
30	56.25	57.50	55.56	59.41	60.43	60.48	57.10	58.78	56.56	56.79	55.00	55.40
40	61.57	62.37	60.84	63.37	63.91	67.40	62.47	62.76	61.80	61.31	60.38	60.80
50	66.64	67.78	66.25	67.96	68.22	71.13	67.38	68.19	67.56	65.87	66.11	66.13
60	71.90	72.70	71.82	71.85	72.34	74.36	72.27	73.36	73.16	71.34	71.46	71.01
70	77.93	78.03	77.79	77.92	79.49	——	77.08	79.56	78.57	77.26	77.67	77.81
80	84.96	86.71	84.90	85.33	86.67	——	85.67	85.78	84.94	84.38	85.25	84.91
90	92.45	92.87	92.45	92.01	93.44	——	93.17	92.87	92.45	91.79	92.01	92.45

* The divisions of the Ecclesall Bierlow district are not always clearly distinguished in the published returns of the mortality, we are therefore compelled, after giving the Township, to state the general results of the mortality of the remainder, or more rural part of the district, which includes the two Hallams, and several small villages or hamlets in Derbyshire.

† The results, with respect to Handsworth, are perhaps to be received with some reserve, the population being small, the data, on which the calculations are founded, are necessarily very limited, particularly at advanced ages.

The foregoing table presents many interesting facts. The average duration of life is shown to be very different in the two registration Districts, and in the several divisions of each. It is higher in Ecclesall Bierlow than in the Sheffield district. Thus the mean ages of persons dying above five years of age, varies in the first six columns as follows: 42.16—43.07—41.81—45.85—43.38—47.31 ; and above every other age which is stated, there are the same differences. In confining the attention to the four divisions of the Sheffield registration district, the duration of life in each is observed to be very dissimilar, evidence of the influence of the several localities on health, arising from differences in the occupations as well as in the density of the population. Thus the mean age of individuals dying above 40 years of age, is in the Sheffield township, 60.84—Brightside Bierlow, 63.37—and in Attercliff-cum-Darnall, 63.91 ; in the two latter divisions, a part of the inhabitants is suburban or rural in character, hence the modifications in the results. In the Handsworth division, in which the inhabitants are chiefly engaged in agricultural pursuits, the mean age above 40 is 67.40.

In the several sub-divisions of the township of Sheffield, where the differences in the circumstances of the inhabitants are much less than in the divisions to which we have alluded, we perceive a closer agreement in the mean duration of life. It appears, however, from facts, the accuracy of which cannot be questioned, that even in the rural portions of the Ecclesall Bierlow district,* in the immediate vicinity of the town, where the inhabitants are

* We beg to thank the intelligent superintendent Registrar of this District, Mr. Benjamin Slater, for his kindness in facilitating our inquiries.

principally engaged in agricultural pursuits, the mean duration of life is comparatively low. The following facts are founded on the four first years of registration :—

	Mean age at decease, of all classes, and both sexes.
Township of Ecclesall Bierlow, of mixed character, one part being oppidan and the other rural....................................	23.09
The more rural part, or the remainder of this district	26.28
The whole district....................................	24.12

The mean duration of life, even in the rural portion of this district, presents no flattering evidence of the healthiness of it. It is considerably less than belongs to the whole of England and Wales, the population of which is unquestionably of a more mixed kind—

England and Wales...........................	29.11
Devonshire	33.01
Birmingham.....................................	24 24
Leeds..	21.24

We were not prepared to find it less than the returns for England and Wales, though certainly much beneath the duration of life in purely agricultural districts. The cause may be thus explained: In the rural districts, for several miles in all directions, taking the town as a centre, a portion of the population is engaged in manufactures, which are sometimes carried on in the country. Even when this is not the case, many of the farmers are manufacturers as well as agriculturists, and only in an humble way in either occupation; they are indeed familiar with hard labour and the struggles and anxieties inseparable from the vicissitudes of trade. The habits of manufacturing towns—the dissipation or luxuries of civilized life, extend, also, for miles, into what would be properly designated the rural districts, and this circumstance, were it closely analysed, would be found to be an important element influencing the health of the inhabitants. And therefore, even in the division of Handsworth, the population of which is more exclusively occupied in the land, than in any other division in the two Registration Districts, to which the calculations in the table refer, it cannot by any means be adduced as an illustration of the rate of mortality in an agricultural population, widely remote from the influence of manufactures.

The mean age at death, taking the entire population of the country generally, has in all probability varied little for an extended series of years. The data, on which the calculations were founded were not always to be depended upon, and even when the general faithfulness of them could not be questioned, they were much more limited than the facts furnished by the present systematic registration. The prevailing opinion is, that the mean duration of life is greater now than in former times, and such perhaps to a slight degree is the case; the figures, however, brought forward in corroboration of the fact, throw no light on the changes in the character of the population. We have no hesitation in asserting, that the sufferings of the working classes, and consequently the rate of mortality, are greater now than in former times. Indeed in most manufacturing districts the rate of mortality in these classes is appalling to contemplate, when it can be studied in reference to them alone, *and not in connexion with the entire population*. The supposed gain on the side of longevity, arises chiefly from two circumstances, a relatively much more numerous middle class than formerly existed, in the possession of the means of comfort and independence, and a better state of morals, or perhaps more correctly speaking, less grossness of dissipation both in the middle and higher classes of society. We question the great improvements in the morals of either class. What they have lost in the grossness of their vices, we fear they have gained in the refinements of hypocrisy and dissimulation. On the surface of society there is less to disgust, but there is much more than formerly to keep awake the most vigilant circumspection in the every day transactions of life. The consideration of this subject almost inclines one to the conclusion, that the vices of mankind are rather modified in character and direction, than diminished in amount, by the constant changes in the condition of society. A man, at the present time, is horror-struck at the bare idea of the gross sensualities of his forefathers, yet feels little compunction in putting in operation the most elaborate system of imposition, so nicely calculated as just to evade the law.

The prevailing tendency of the times, is to make the exterior man as unlike the interior as possible, and the attempt presents numerous instances of exquisite success. An individual, who was unfortunate in his circumstances fifty years ago, rarely rose again into credit or public estimation, especially if any doubt were cast upon the honesty of his conduct. Now, insolvency conjoined with very questionable integrity, does not materially affect his position, if he only take care—which apparently is no difficult matter, certainly no uncommon one, to keep up the same establishment and the same appearances as before. If he fail to do this, he is at once damned, and sinks into general contempt.

The concentrated feeling of the present age, in this country particularly, is the adoration of wealth. This embodies every virtue, and is associated with every talent. Religion seems not, in any degree, to modify the thirst for it, or to abate the ardour of the pursuit. The love of the world grows with the contemplation of things above.

The following facts are interesting, showing the rate of mortality at different periods :—

	Mean age at death of the whole population.
London, from Bills of mortality, 1796	29.03
———————————— 1810	27.51
———————————— 1813-30 (18 yrs)	30.07
Aggregate mean of these 20 years..................	29.89
Two first years of Registration, 1837-8-9	28.18
The mean age at death of all who died at 40 and upwards, during the first named twenty years, in the metropolis	61.50
The same average from the two first years of Registration	61.65

In pursuing the inquiry into the subject of mortality, we have been led to perceive an imperfection in the general system of registration. In regard to completeness, and the amount of valuable information which it furnishes, it is immeasurably superior to any means previously employed: there is, however, a defect in it, of the importance of which our investigations have made us duly sensible. The births and the deaths are recorded without stating to what class of society they belong, consequently, the results are too general to throw any definite light on the changes in the condition of each class.

It is an interesting question, to determine the influence of poverty and riches on the increase of mankind, but it is evident, that unless we have the particular births to each class, we have not the data from which to draw precise conclusions. The gross results may be compared with similar results at other periods, and, in connexion with the obvious changes in the condition of society, will furnish much important matter for consideration. It is quite possible, however, that a large portion of the difference in the results, viewed as illustrative of the gradual improvement in the condition of society, may be owing chiefly to the bettering of the condition of one class. The information will clearly not allow us to state what are the changes in each.

There are few questions in political economy more pregnant with interest, than the influence of circumstances on the multiplication of the human species, and the curious and unexpected results which have been arrived at, by some recent inquirers, show how desirable it is that the fullest information should be possessed on the subject. Without such discrimination, in recording what belongs to each class, the facts establishing the rate of mortality will lose much of their value. Were it stated in reference to each, it would be a correct measure of the physical condition of each, and would show accurately the influence of particular circumstances on the duration of life, such as the modifications in manufacturing pursuits from the introduction of machinery—the multiplication in the diversities of employment—the extension of manufactures—the effects of periods of prosperity and adversity, and the influence of changes in the prices of provisions; and, lastly, how far a command of the comforts or luxuries of life affects the duration of human existence. The consideration of these matters would be attended with little difficulty, were the mortality of each class accurately stated. As evidence of the importance of such information, we may remark, that the deaths in the three classes, the *upper*, the *middle* and the *lower*, are

given for the borough of Leeds, and the following are the
results in relation to each, exhibiting an astounding difference in the value of life :—

Mean age at Death.

Of the Upper classes 44
       Middle   27
       Lower 19*

Such is the difference in the mean age of all who die
in these classes, and which will illustrate the force of our
remarks respecting the advantage, indeed the necessity of
such information, in treating of the subject of mortality in
reference to the influence of local as well as general
circumstances.   The three classes, though intimately
associated, are not so bound together that an aggravation
in the sufferings of one, for example the lower classes, will
be accompanied with a change in the others, affecting to a
corresponding extent the duration of life. On the contrary,
it is not only possible, but probable, that when the mortality
is the greatest in the lower classes, from long continued
distress, it may be the least in the two other classes. The
scarcity of money, and the consequent economy which is
put in practice, by parties who have a command of the
luxuries of life, tends, by correcting excesses and sensual
indulgences, to diminish the rate of mortality : thus the
gross returns upon the three classes, will convey no exact
knowledge of the condition of each. We may be deceived
by them into the belief, that society is gradually improving
in its physical and social condition, when indeed the most
numerous class may be stationary, or in the process of
deterioration.

* The *aggregate* average of these three ages is 21 years.

The required information on this subject, would be furnished without any additional expence, and with very little trouble to those engaged in the practical duties of registration. Every registration district is divided into minor districts, in each of which the person employed records the births and deaths, and an extra column would enable him to state, whether the birth or the death belonged to the *higher*, the *middle*, or the *lower* classes. All that is necessary, as a preparatory step, is to define clearly the condition of the individuals so classified, which would certainly be no difficult matter. We strongly urge the importance of these remarks, and hope they will induce those, on whom the superintendance of the registration depends, if not in the highest quarters, at least in manufacturing districts, where the population is subject to serious vicissitudes in the demand for labour, to furnish this additional information.

CHAPTER IX.

THE SAVINGS' BANK.

There is no public institution possessing a higher claim on our consideration, in connexion with the scope of this inquiry, than that which receives the surplus means of the industrious and provident artisan. By some, it has been regarded as indicating accurately the state of trade, its funds being supposed to rise and fall with the periodical or frequent vicissitudes of commerce. Such a correspondence would naturally be inferred. The deposits, however, do not fluctuate in amount with the changes in trade, but, on the contrary, have been nearly stationary during the present period of severe depression.

It is questionable whether prosperity be as conducive to their augmentation as adversity. The one begets extravagance, thoughtlessness and a disregard of the future. The other, by teaching the value of money, excites economical considerations, not only in the artisan, strictly so designated, but in persons whose income is, perhaps, little influenced by the more or less healthy state of manufactures.

Previously to investigation, we imagined the funds of the institution were affected by the existing conditions of trade, but finding such not to be borne out by facts, we have been led to the examination of the character or occupations of the numerous depositors. The inquiry has been one of considerable difficulty and labour. The results furnished, show how small a proportion of the artisans are depositors, hence their ˙condition, whether prosperous or otherwise, will clearly exercise little influence on the amount of the deposits. When the average stability of employment in any branch is known, as well as the average remuneration which it affords, it will be easy and interesting to trace the connexion between such circumstances and the habits of provident calculation. The Savings' Bank is peculiarly fitted to receive the surplus means of the artisan. He may deposit the smallest sum, and can withdraw it at once, without being put to any inconvenience or expense. His hard earnings are not only safe, but are returned to him with the addition of interest.

The following Table gives the number of Depositors, and the amount deposited under or above certain sums, for five years in succession, and it is remarkable how little variation is observed in them, during which period trade has been exceedingly depressed:—

DEPOSITORS	1838	1839	1840	1841	1842	TOTAL AMOUNT OF EACH CLASS 1838 (£ s. d.)	1839 (£ s. d.)	1840 (£ s. d.)	1841 (£ s. d.)	1842 (£ s. d.)
Whose respective balances did not exceed £20 each	2720	2780	2856	2978	2791	21553 1 7	18506 5 0	19503 1 0	19951 1 3	20059 13 6
Whose respective balances were above £20 and not exceeding £50	1386	1406	1476	1396	1469	42841 4 9	43504 17 0	45996 13 1	46000 17 5	46069 5 2
Whose respective balances were above £50 and not exceeding £100	609	605	600	614	599	41387 6 11	41547 10 6	42313 3 3	45983 5 2	41698 1 2
Whose respective balances were above £100 and not exceeding £150	199	207	223	256	223	22530 16 4	24760 4 5	26552 16 4	28027 11 1	27565 6 8
Whose respective balances were above £150 and not exceeding £200	83	86	89	97	90	13111 2 4	13570 8 3	14028 16 6	12546 15 1	16175 8 11
Whose respective balances exceeded £200	5	5	4	6	6	1270 16 6	1139 3 10	871 4 9	646 14 6	2617 14 11
Total number of depositors	4993	5088	5948	5174	5197	142844 8 5	143098 9 0	148534 14 11	153056 4 6	159115 10 4
Charitable Societies	8	8	6	11	12	473 6 7	848 3 9	631 5 1	705 15 10	707 10 0
Friendly Societies	45	32	30	40	48	9442 13 3	8597 16 10	9194 12 8	9207 16 4	8347 10 3
Total number of depositors	5046	5128	5984	5224	5257	152760 8 3	152534 9 7	158360 12 8	161905 16 8	162170 10 7

Male Depositors and their Occupations, in the year 1840.

Anvil makers	2	Fender makers...	7	Painters	15
Artist	1	Farmers & men...	125	Press cutters	3
Auctioneer	1	Fork makers	30	Powder flask mkrs	4
Architect	1	Filesmiths	94	Plumbers	2
Boatmen	4	Forgemen	24	Pattern card makr	1
Butchers	24	Flask maker	1	Printers	4
Bookseller	1	Fruiterers	2	Postboys	4
Brushmakers	7	Gamekeepers	4	Postman	1
Brace bit makers,	2	Glaziers	4	Paper makers	2
Brass turners	9	Grinders(various)	119	Razorsmiths	23
Blacksmiths	35	Gardeners	37	Rule maker	1
Bookkeepers	80	Glover	1	Roller men	18
Brewery men	14	Grocers	15	Rope maker	2
Brickmakers	5	Glass maker	1	Silk dyer	1
Bakers	5	Haft pressers	10	Steel melters	38
Basket makers	2	Hostlers	4	Skinners	3
Cutlers (various)..	221	Harness makers..	2	Sawyers	9
Cabinet makers...	19	Hair dressers	12	Schoolmasters	18
Coal leaders	13	Hay dealer	1	Saw handle mkrs.	9
Cast steel burners	2	Hatters	5	Stove grate mkrs.	13
Colliers	61	Joiners	55	Shearsmiths	5
Coopers	9	Joiners' tool mkrs	5	Scythe & sickle makers	45
Collector	1	Inkstand maker..	1		
Confectioners	10	Ironmongers	4	Spectacle frame maker	1
Clockmakers	2	Labourers	201		
Carpenters	5	Lime burner	1	Servants (men)...	153
Coachmakers	8	Locksmith	1	Shopkeepers	8
Comb makers	7	Lancet maker	1	Silver platers	89
Coachmen	11	Ivory cutters	6	Scissorsmiths	44
Curriers	12	Moulders	34	Scale cutters & Pressers	15
Cow keepers	11	Masons	43		
Diesinkers	11	Miners	15	Shoemakers	71
Druggists	3	Millers (men)	22	Saw makers	34
Drapers	6	Metalsmiths	25	Slaters	3
Dentist	1	Mark makers	4	Stampers	2
Edge tool makers	25	Musicians	3	Spade maker	1
Excisemen	6	Millwrights	10	Stoker	1
Engravers	9	Machine maker...	1	Saddlers	4
Engineers and keepers	13	Nail makers	10	Soap boiler	1
		Opticians	9	Spade shaft mkrs.	4
Fishmongers	3	Plasterers	2	Spindle makers...	4

Tilters 12   Wood turners ... 4   Watchmakers ... 2
Type founders ... 15   Waiter 1   Waggoners 1
Table knife forgrs 17   Warehousemen... 15   Victuallers 26
Tailors 54   Whitesmiths 10   Infants 323
Turners............ 11   Weavers 4
Travellers 7   Wheelwrights ... 13   Male depositors 2,716
Wire drawers ... 3   Woodmen......... 3

Female Depositors with their Occupations.

Bonnet makers... 15   Silver burnishers 5   Widows 213
Dressmakers...... 75   Schoolmistresses, 25   Infants 387
Governesses 7   Servants 650
Housekeepers ... 84   Shopkeepers 38   Female depo- ⎫
Mangle keepers .. 2   Washerwomen ... 5   sitors ......⎬ 1,870
Nurses 2   Women (married)362   ⎭

Summary.

Male depositors 2,716
Female depositors 1,870
Sick clubs, Charitable institution and Trust moneys......... 436

Total number of depositors 5,022

The artisans do not form, according to these returns, the principal part of the depositors. The following are the most important branches of trade carried on in this town and neighbourhood, employing collectively many thousand workmen, and to each branch is annexed the number of depositors :—

Anvil makers ... 2   Joiners' tool mkrs 5   Scissorsmiths ... 44
Cutlers (various)..221   Moulders 34   Scale pressers ... 15
Edge tool makers 25   Metalsmiths 25   Saw makers 34
Fender makers... 7   Opticians 9   Spindle makers... 4
Fork makers...... 30   Razorsmiths 23   Tilters 12
Filesmiths....,... 94   Roller men 18   Type founders ... 5
Forgemen .,....... 24   Steel melters...... 38   Table knife forgrs 17
Flask makers ... 5   Stove grate mkrs. 13
Grinders 119   Scythe makers ... 45   Total 967
Haft pressers ... 10   Silver platers ... 89

The number of cutlers is above 5000, and yet there are only 221 depositors. Reasons may certainly be assigned for this small proportion. The various branches of the cutlery manufacture are exceedingly liable to fluctuations, and it is perhaps questionable, whether the demand for several consecutive months, is ever fully equal to the ability to produce. The different branches of it are overstocked, and none, except first-rate workmen, engaged in the making of fine or costly articles, are remunerated in such a manner, as to be enabled to secure a provision for the future. In striking contrast with this department of trade, the silver plated manufacture may be mentioned. The number of workmen employed is from 450 to 500, and yet this small number furnishes 89 depositors. The greatest proportion is found amongst the best paid artisans, as forgemen, edge tool makers, steel melters, scythe and saw makers; and yet even in these branches, the number, calculating on the necessities of the future, is miserably small. In our opinion, the principles on which Savings' Banks are established, are not well understood by the labouring classes.

There is an impression on the minds of many, that these institutions originate with Government, and are instruments in their hands for purposes not yet apparent. It is remarkable how very slightly the number of depositors and the amount deposited, differ in the years 1838 and 1839. The depositors in the latter were 82 more than in the former, and the amount deposited less by £25 18s. 8d. Both years were periods of great commercial distress, and which indeed had existed from the latter part of 1836; it was therefore reasonable to expect, that if the number of depositors, or the amount deposited, were greatly influenced

by the state of trade, a serious reduction in both would be
constantly observed during the depression.

The condition of the Savings' Banks has been alluded
to in Parliament, as evidence that the prevailing distress is
exaggerated. We do not consider such institutions an
accurate test of the circumstances of the labouring classes.
They present no fluctuations corresponding with changes
in the demand for labour, or the scale of its remuneration.

It is pleasing to remark the great number of female
servants as depositors. They are 650 in 5022, being as
one to eight, nearly. The number of servant men is 153,
and of labourers, 201. Few of these can be supposed to
be in the receipt of large wages, and yet collectively they
form about one-fifth part of the total depositors. From
these facts we are disposed to infer, that it is rather the
disposition than the ability, which is wanting, in the
majority of the artisans, at least during a moderate state of
trade, to reserve a portion of their surplus means. The
necessity, as well as the advantage of such conduct, is
taught by distress and hence it is, that under such circumstances, the funds are increased, or at least remain
stationary, which can only be explained on the principle
here stated. Necessity at such times must compel
many to withdraw their deposits, or a large portion of
them, and if not replaced by others, stimulated in an
equal ratio, by the spirit of economy, the funds would
clearly ebb and flow with the changes of the times.

The returns of the number of depositors and the amount
deposited for 1840-1-2, were procured subsequently to the
foregoing remarks. It was stated, by competent authorities,

that in 1840, distress among the artisans was greater than at any period since 1836, and this is corroborated by the greater amount paid to casual poor, which is the least exceptionable of all evidence. The two subsequent years, however, 1841 and 1842, have been accompanied with still further aggravated suffering and struggling to all classes. The existing distress has been greatly increased by the failure of the oldest Bank in the town, Parker, Shore, and Co., an event as unexpected as the justly high character of the parties was above suspicion.* In the latter year, 1842, the greatest number of able-bodied men was out of employment, and the poor-rates were exceedingly heavy; yet we perceive no important changes either in the number of depositors or the amount deposited, compared with preceding years. Indeed the amount deposited is the greatest in the past year, and, also, with one exception, the number of depositors.

From these facts it is evident, that the condition of the Savings' Bank of this town affords no indication whatever of the more or less prosperous state of manufactures, or of the circumstances of the artisans generally. Economy and the necessity of providing for the future, are lessons not only best taught by times of adversity, but are always more fully acted upon than in periods of commercial prosperity.

* In alluding to the misfortunes of this firm, the character—the services and the position of the two leading partners demand a few remarks. Perhaps no two persons ever stood higher, or more justly, in the estimation of the town, than Mr. Hugh Parker and Mr. Offley Shore. Their time, purse and talents were always at the service of the public, and there was no charity or object of good but what received their support. Their misfortunes arose, not from reckless or gambling speculations, but from carrying into business transactions, the liberality which distinguished them in private life.

CHAPTER X.

MORAL STATE OF THE POPULATION.

Crime, immorality and vicious habits are evils generally attendant on manufactures, and it is difficult to devise any measures calculated to correct them. The philanthropist, abounding in good intentions, and ardent to put his beneficent schemes in practice, is frequently very imperfectly acquainted with the nature of the evils and the circumstances by which they are aggravated. He perceives clearly what he wishes to effect, but does not understand fully the obstacles in the way of his efforts. We are not less anxious than he to ameliorate the existing misery and the widely pervading ignorance of the labouring classes; we are less sanguine, perhaps, in our anticipations of success from any system of legislation, except that which diffuses knowledge and diminishes the hours of labour. To offer the one, without the accompaniment of the other, would be a mockery of kindly consideration.

We were cradled in the midst of manufactures, and have long studied their influence on society. We are not insensible of the immense good which they confer—the large and princely fortunes which they create—the encouragement which they give to the arts—the enterprise and energy which they excite—the liberalizing tendencies with which they are fraught—the just and comprehensive views which they develope of the relations of man to man, and the various elegancies and refined enjoyments which they diffuse around. This, however, is only one side of the picture. The other, the artisan, engaged in the production of national wealth, presents phases and circumstances less flattering to our pride, and much less grateful to contemplate. They are too graphic in their character to be overlooked, and too important to be neglected Among the numerous causes, which appear inseparable from manufactures, producing crime and immorality, the following deserve particular notice:—

1. The crowding together of the working classes into narrow streets, filthy lanes, alleys and yards, is a serious evil, and one which has hitherto increased in all manufacturing towns; nor is it easy to imagine, how it can be corrected by the judicious suggestions or well directed efforts of local authorities. Some of its consequences may be ameliorated. Attention to paving, drainage and sewerage will diminish the unhealthiness of such places, but how to touch the gross ignorance and wretchedness in which they abound, is a problem exceedingly difficult to solve. The lamentable condition of the masses in such situations is the result of causes over which local authorities have no control, such as the necessarily precarious nature of employment—the fitful extremes of remuneration,—at one moment insufficient to purchase the common necessaries of life, at another, gratifying the gross indulgences of the appetite.

The poor are not resident in these places from choice, but from necessity. Families are not huddled together into dark, ill ventilated rooms from any peculiar pleasure which it affords ; they may indeed have become insensible of the inconvenience and wretchedness of such situations, but slender and uncertain means do not enable them to command more comfortable abodes. They are fixed there by circumstances.

2. It is the nature of manufactures to fluctuate. A period of prosperity invariably begets one of adversity ; and as inevitably does the latter lead to the former. Long continued good trade gives full employment and enhanced remuneration, and stimulates production, until at length it exceeds the necessities of both home and foreign markets. During a season of excessive demand, the artisan riots in the affluence of his means, and his conduct is frequently marked by dissipation, neglect of work, and a disregard of the certain necessities of the future. This state of things, which seems inevitable, is prejudicial in the extreme to his mental, moral and physical improvement. His conduct is not only baneful in its influence on himself, but on all who depend upon him. His children, to enable him to support his dissipation, are put to work at a tender age, with little, if any education, and thus one generation succeeds another with the same vicious tendencies. Commercial adversity has in its train evils much more aggravated in character, penury, suffering and wretchedness in every possible form. The want of employment is felt not only by the improvident ;—the honest and industrious artisan breaks down in the struggle to live—his independence and self-respect are gradually lost, and when he ceases to command a miserable pittance for his labour, as a last

resource, he applies to the parish for relief. Returning prosperity cannot place him in his former position—cannot give him back his former independent or moral tone of mind. These are the evils which spring out of the vicissitudes of trade—out of the periodical changes in the demand for labour, and they will ever occur, whatever be the form of governments or the wisdom of legislation.

3. The early employment of children in manufactures is incompatible with the steady improvement of the artisan. The injurious influence of this circumstance is perceived in many of the branches carried on in this town. In those in which the young are early put to work, there is a remarkable difference between the intelligence, morality and independence of the workmen, and the artisans in branches in which the young are seldom admitted under fourteen years of age. Many facts, in confirmation of this, are given in the analysis of the several trades in a subsequent part of this inquiry.

4. Another circumstance, fraught with much evil and worthy of notice, is the employment of girls and women in manufactories. The introduction of them has greatly increased, of late years, in all branches in which they can be made useful. In the majority of instances, both sexes work in the same room, and are under no particular superintendance. It will readily be admitted, that a workshop is a very indifferent school for the future wife, the duties of which are usually undertaken at an early age.

To every person acquainted with manufactures, it is manifest, that one of the great and growing evils, unfavourable to the progress of morality and intelligence, is the extent to which females are employed in workshops. The influence of this circumstance extends widely, and counteracts much of the good that education would otherwise produce. The frequent associations which in consequence take place among the sexes in very early life—the vicious habits which are formed, and the marriages which result, with little thought or provision for the future, render the domestic hearth not one of comfort to the husband, nor a school of virtue to the children. Ignorance, wretchedness, and dissipation, are the evils which spring luxuriantly out of such circumstances, and are multiplied in the successive generations.

The progress of civilization must not be measured by the creation of wealth, nor does the latter afford a just indication of the amount of happiness pervading society. The intensity of the struggle to accumulate riches, is familiar with disappointments and anxieties, and is too apt to exert a painful degree of pressure on the millions—the instruments in the process. The imposing expression of independence and affluence in the few, must not mislead us in our estimate of the condition of the many. To appreciate this, we must take into consideration the urgent difficulties experienced by the masses, to procure the common necessaries of life, the melancholy failure of the attempt, as shewn by the appalling fact, that in many manufacturing districts, from one-seventh to one-tenth of the population is dependent altogether on parochial relief. And how large a proportion, at the same time, equally suffering, of whom we have no record, is dragging on a miserable existence! Further evidence in support of the same view may be drawn from our crowded prisons, becoming indeed immense establishments in the land. There

never was a period in the history of this country, or, perhaps of the world, in which the same amount of indigence
and crime existed, in relation to the population, and in
association with boundless wealth, inactive and unprofitable,
or overflowing in the refined indulgences of a selfish and
luxurious age.

The employment of girls and women, is both an effect
and cause of this state of things, and though there are
evils which the legislature cannot remove, this is one which
admits of considerable correction. The town council of
Leeds, in their statistical inquiry, remark, in allusion to
this subject :—" Take, on the other hand, a mill girl from
" the town ; she leaves her work and hastens to her asso-
" ciates, with whom, during the day, she has planned some
" project for the evening ; her father is at the public house ;
" her mother, thus left for months, has herself become
" careless in her person, and almost reckless in her habits ;
" the daughter thus has no one to guide her, her associates
" at home and abroad are abandoned, eventually she
" becomes so herself, and is lost to all sense of decency."*

This is not an overcharged picture, and it certainly
exhibits evils annually augmenting, and which must considerably neutralize all benevolent attempts to improve
the condition of the working classes. We will not add
darker touches to the picture by describing the situation of
the shop girl when destitute of employment. They may
be forcibly imagined, and will lose nothing by our silence.

Persons, little familiar with manufacturing pursuits, are
apt to regard the vices and irregularities of the working
classes, as originating entirely in themselves, and lose sight,

* Page 17.

in the harshness of their judgment, of the trying and painful circumstances in which they are placed.

In the foregoing remarks, we have dwelt on some of the evils inevitably attendant on manufactures, and none are so important as the fluctuations which are inherent in them. The changes in the condition of the artisan, whether arising from prosperity or adversity, are almost equally unfavourable to his progressive improvement in morality or intelligence. When he begins life ignorant of the elements of knowledge—has been familiar with labour from his tenderest years, and has not even had the advantage of example or precept, to teach him the value of good deeds, it is expecting too much of human nature, to anticipate that he will be virtuous and provident in prosperity, or sternly independent in adversity. Extremes are severe trials to all men, and to the uneducated it is difficult to resist the tendencies to which they lead.

Among the evils under which the masses in this country particularly labour, and which admits of redress, is the want of a comprehensive system of education, and of judicious restrictions on the employment of the young. Let the masses have light, otherwise they will become fearful elements of discord. So imperative is this necessity—so urgent are the demands of the times, that it becomes us, to waive the absorbing importance attached to doctrinal distinctions—distinctions dividing man from his fellow man, and to unite, as if we felt a common interest in the improvement of mankind. Let us not urge in bitterness the severity of exclusive sentiments, but endeavour, in the largeness of a liberal spirit, to elevate the intellectual and moral condition of the people, impressed with this conviction, that if our peculiar views alone be right, the field on which we wish to exhibit them will not be narrowed by the more general diffusion of information. Nor let us entertain the apprehension, that any proposed system, which may be regarded as working too much in one direction, will be so efficient in its application that no immorality will remain to be corrected. With the best intentions on the part of the legislature, and with the earnest desire of all, on whom the carrying out of these intentions rests, society will still abound in vice, ignorance and grovelling tendencies.

We have modified the system of relief in relation to the indigent poor, to prevent the higher and the middle classes from being swallowed up in the growing degradation and necessities of the masses. We have enlarged our prisons for the reception of felons, and we have increased the facilities for insolvent debtors, so that now, it is as easy to get quit of obligations as to incur them, and all these changes were demanded by the times. Do not these facts speak eloquently of the necessity of a comprehensive system of education, in harmony, also, with the urgent necessities of the times ?   Are we to exhibit almost a unanimity of sentiment, when it is proposed to reduce the claims of the poor, to build and enlarge prisons, and so to modify legislation in regard to insolvency, that the debtor has little difficulty in paying the creditor—according to law ; and yet when it is proposed to educate the poor, we are at once in arms, afraid that they will be enlightened and made good according to an established system, when the great truths of this system are the common truths on which all believers rest ?

L

The consideration of this subject would almost lead us to regret, that we have looked to remote regions for a field, on which religion might exercise her influence and teach important truths, when the millions at our own door were vicious in their habits, wretched in their condition, and ignorant, not only of spiritual truths, but of the simplest rudiments of knowledge. In the transactions of private life, it is possible to be generous before we are just, and the same error may show itself in the expansive wish and ardent zeal that lose themselves in the contemplation of human degradation at a distance. We honour the benevolence that comprehends the universe in its view, but the first duty of benevolence, is to study the wants of mankind at home.

The following tables elucidate the state of crime and immorality in the town of Sheffield. The first gives the number, ages and sex of those committed for trial on the charge of felony, from 1834 to 1842. The second, the same information, and for the same period, of those conveyed to the police office as disorderly, by which term is understood misconduct of some kind, often petty theft—persons taken under suspicious circumstances, but evidence wanting to convict them, and aggravated cases of abuse arising from intoxication. The third, gives, also, the same information and for the same period, of vagrants, which term is somewhat comprehensive. It includes stubborn or insolent beggars,—impostors,—individuals of questionable character unable to give a satisfactory account of themselves, or charged with crimes not deemed of sufficient importance to commit them for trial.

NUMBER OF PERSONS COMMITTED FOR TRIAL.

YEAR.	AGE OF MALES.				AGE OF FEMALES				Total Number of Males.	Total Number of Females.	Total Number of Males & Females
	Under 20.	20 to 30.	30 to 50.	50, and upwards.	Under 20.	20 to 30.	30 to 50.	50, and upwards.			
1834*	14	98	28	...	17	17	...	...	140	34	174
1835	24	119	35	...	14	13	...	...	178	27	205
1836	29	110	33	...	8	16	4	...	172	28	200
1837	34	186	71	...	7	19	...	...	291	26	317
1838	100	114	8	5	16	9	...	...	227	25	252
1839	58	177	10	2	21	29	...	...	247	50	297
1840	41	54	21	...	5	7	5	...	116	17	133
1841	31	44	12	1	6	11	4	1	88	22	110
1842	44	96	26	8	6	18	6	1	174	31	205

* From April to December only.

From the preceding table it appears that crime has increased in a much greater ratio than the population, whether we take into consideration that of the township or the parish. In the former, the population in 1835 was 64,569, the number committed for trial, 205. In 1839, the population was 68,408, and the number committed was 297. Thus while population had increased six per cent., crime increased absolutely forty-six per cent.; or relatively to the augmented population, thirty-eight per cent., which is the just mode of calculation.

In examining the commitments from 1839 to 1842, an individual unacquainted with such matters, would imagine that an immense improvement had taken place in the morals of the people, the number having greatly decreased in the three subsequent years. The cause which explains this, shows how little figures are, in many instances, to be depended upon, except in connexion with particular circumstances unreservedly stated. The *decrease* in figures, paradoxical as it may appear, becomes somewhat a measure

L 2

of the *increase* of immorality. Crimes of the same kind, and in all respects equally injurious to society, are not treated, at different periods, with the same severity of punishment. A much greater proportion, at one time, is committed for trial than at another, and this arises, indeed, from a curious circumstance. We are sorry it cannot be ascribed to the better informed judgments of the magistrates, or to a desire on their part to try the effects of lenient measures, *but to the fact, that the prison to which the felons would be sent, is too crowded to admit them in any thing like the proportion of less distressed times.*

This is the statement of the magistrates themselves made to one of the Assistant Commissioners,* who recently visited this town, in order to report concerning the general condition of it. There is evidence of its truth in the following table. While the number of commitments for trial exhibits a decrease, the number of the disorderlies shows an augmentation. Many, that would under ordinary circumstances, be included in the first table are placed in the second, and, after some confinement in the prison of the town, which is only for their temporary accommodation, are dismissed without having been brought before the bench, and others after a severe reprimand. Hence we perceive, that the number of disorderlies in 1841, is greater by 547 than in 1838, and the past year shows only a slight diminution in the amount. Without these explanations and comparisons, such returns would be of little value. The causes which influence the numerical strength of one class, will equally modify that of another, though the tables may not clearly show this, unless viewed in relation to each other, according to the facts which have been stated. The returns are affected by the times, and, it would appear to a

* J. C. Symons, Esq.

very great extent, reasoning on the disorderlies in different years—a class which is exceedingly comprehensive, including every shade of roguery, from the incorrigible thief to the unfortunate drunkard. In 1835 trade generally was particularly good, and the disorderlies were 1009, while in the two past years, they have increased two-fold, during which, unprecedented suffering has pervaded the masses of the population. These facts are full of instruction, and show how important it is, to endeavour to counteract the growing degradation, not by the enlargement of prisons, but by judicious and liberal measures of education.

Crime is unquestionably on the increase independently of the depression of the times. The causes are in some degree, inseparable from manufactures: the legislature, however, has important duties to perform in relation to the population, which, taking into consideration the influence which it might legitimately exercise, have been lamentably neglected. The laws have permitted and facilitated the accumulation of large fortunes, but have not made these subservient to education.

The causes are fluctuations in the rate of wages, at one period, so high, as to generate idleness and dissipation; at another, too low to afford the common necessaries of life. With the advancement of manufactures, competition in all branches is aggravated—the effect of which is to diminish profits, to put the bodily and mental energies on the full stretch, and, the intensity of the struggle brings into requisition a gradually increasing proportion of children and females. The latter is an inevitable result of reckless competitive exertions, and will always be a formidable evil, tending to counteract the wisest and most practical of legislative measures towards the mental improvement of the population.

TABLE OF THE DISORDERLIES.

YEAR.	AGE OF MALES.				AGE OF FEMALES.				Total Number of Males.	Total Number of Females.	Total Number of Males & Females
	Under 20.	20 to 30.	30 to 50.	50, and upwards.	Under 20.	20 to 30.	30 to 50.	50, and upwards.			
1834*	69	337	116	7	23	38	6	2	529	69	598
1835	170	532	197	30	15	57	3	5	929	80	1009
1836	213	683	327	55	45	57	30	14	1278	146	1424
1837	199	777	385	90	41	82	40	10	1451	173	1624
1838	210	715	310	84	44	83	39	11	1319	177	1496
1839	357	787	344	87	35	105	44	11	1575	195	1770
1840	132	621	484	77	45	103	48	13	1314	209	1523
1841	311	856	524	127	64	196	66	9	1818	325	2143
1842	286	781	560	98	61	188	55	11	1725	315	2040

* From April to December only.

TABLE OF VAGRANTS.

YEAR.	AGE OF MALES.				AGE OF FEMALES.				Total Number of Males.	Total Number of Females.	Total Number of Males & Females
	Under 20.	20 to 30.	30 to 50.	50, and upwards.	Under 20.	20 to 30.	30 to 50.	50, and upwards.			
1834*	9	18	2	...	4	4	3	1	29	12	4
1835	30	35	4	2	5	8	3	...	71	11	82
1836	33	25	7	...	7	8	1	...	65	16	81
1837	54	55	9	2	8	17	2	1	120	28	148
1838	52	34	6	1	12	9	1	...	93	22	115
1839	27	33	7	2	5	7	1	. 1	69	14	83
1840	42	41	10	...	6	8	2	1	93	17	110
1841	31	40	19	2	6	4	8	...	92	18	110
1842	63	41	18	4	20	15	3	1	126	39	165

* From April to December only.

We regret that these tables are not more complete. The trade of the individual, the character of the offence and the times they have been committed, would be instructive results. The degree of education possessed by the offenders, whether felons, disorderlies, or vagrants, should also be stated; and we trust that, in future, the returns will be improved by this additional information. The Police Superintendent* is an exceedingly intelligent, active and enterprising officer, and has rendered the establishment over which he presides, admirable for its order and efficiency. To the Magistrates, who have for a series of years, devoted their time and talents to the public service, with strict impartiality and integrity, and whose honourable conduct has always been above suspicion, the town owes a heavy debt of gratitude. To select any from the body, on whom to make a particular remark, would be invidious, but misfortunes, and half a century of labours on the bench, make a demand on our sympathy and impel the expression of our opinion. Let us not forget the services of one†—his solicitude to do justice—his unwearied exertions—his urbane and conciliatory conduct. Let not the claims of the past be forgotten in difficulties and sufferings, in which he participates in common with others,—in his case, to the extent of the loss of his entire fortune.

* Mr. Thomas Raynor.

† Hugh Parker, Esq., late of Woodthorpe.

CHAPTER XI.

SILVER AND PLATED MANUFACTURE.

———

In the following pages, we bring under consideration several important and extensive trades carried on in this town. It is not possible, within the necessarily limited extent of this inquiry, to treat of every department of manufacture. In the selection, we have been principally guided by their importance, in regard to the capital and number of artisans employed, and the very different conditions of the branches, whether we consider the rate of remuneration, intelligence, education and respectability of the workmen, or the regulations of the unions, by which many of these trades are governed. In these several points of view, there is matter worthy of reflection, and which might be shewn to be of practical value to the political economist. To discuss some of them, would, however, be to awaken angry feelings, which we have no desire to call into play. A word breathed indirectly in favour of unions or combinations, is to excite, in the breast of the manufacturer the most perturbed sensations. It is natural to dislike that by which we are controlled, and difficult to persuade us that the influence exercised is to our advantage or that of the public. We all love freedom, which, properly defined, means to do as *we* like, which is often to make others do as *they* do not like. In these inquiries, we have nevertheless a duty to perform, viz. to state facts unreservedly in connexion •with the different branches of trade, and we are not stepping out of our legitimate province, in pointing out the importance of these facts in relation either to the manufacturer or the artisan. We must not be regarded as partisans, but in the light of expositors. We have no interest, either direct or indirect, to consult, nor are we animated by any consideration, except that of rigid impartiality.

This town is more particularly known abroad for its articles of cutlery than for any other branch of manufacture; it is, however, not less celebrated, at home, for its silver and silver-plated productions. In the one case, the widely extended fame arises from the goods being largely exported, while in the other, they are almost wholly consumed in this country. In evidence of this fact the two are not equally subject to the same extreme vicissitudes of prosperity and adversity. During the past six years, distress and embarrassment have been felt, in an aggravated form, by all engaged in the cutlery branches; while in the silver and plated manufactures, until within two years, employment has been steady and wages good. The taste and quality of the articles are, perhaps, not equalled in the world, and the town has no competitor in this department of trade, in regard to the exquisite beauty of elaborate workmanship— the costly and gorgeous character of the goods. One of

the chief causes of this distinguished pre-eminence, is the
respectability, integrity and enterprise of the masters,
conjoined with the command of ample means. Birmingham
is a competitor in the production of cheap and showy
articles, but we stand alone in taste and quality. It is
from this town that London is supplied with the richest
specimens of silver and plated manufactures. The following table shows the value of British made plate, plated
ware, jewellery and watches exported for a series of years.
It must also be borne in mind, that the goods exported are
mostly of the inferior quality :—

1829	£177,830.
1830	190,515.
1831	188,144.
1832	173,593.
1833	179,283.
1834	192,269.
1835	231,903.

The annual consumption of these goods, in this country,
is estimated at £1,200,000. To ascertain the condition of
this important branch of trade, more especially the moral,
physical and intellectual state of the workmen employed,
the subjoined questions were submitted to one of the most
intelligent and enterprising manufacturers, and the accompanying answers were kindly furnished :—

1. What are the distinct branches of this trade?

Designing, modelling, die-cutting and chasing, may be considered
    as one branch; though there are not many die cutters, who
    can chase, or chasers who can cut dies. The remainder may be
    divided into stampers, brasiers, pierced workers, and candle-
    stick makers. There are also, generally, an engine-man, a
    spinner, who works at the lathe, one or two cutters-out, work
    which is sometimes partly performed by the master; one or

two polishers, and one or two who are called supernumeraries. The burnishing is always done by women, and one woman is usually employed as a scourer.

2. What parts are usually executed by adults, and what by apprentices?

There is no branch of this business executed entirely by boys or girls: the boys work at the simpler parts of the work, along with their masters, or those appointed to teach them, and, after an apprenticeship of about seven years, become journeymen; the girls, after three years apprenticeship, become burnishers.

3. Are women employed in any of the branches; and in what proportion to the men?

Women are always employed as burnishers, and sometimes as polishers. The burnishing room is always separate from those in which the men work, and is often in a separate building, over the counting house or warehouse. In a certain manufactory, which may be taken as a sample, there are sixteen women and girls, to fifty-six men and nine boys.

4. What is the proportion of apprentices to adults, in the several branches; and at what age are they usually put to work?

This question is partly answered above. Formerly, i.e. fifteen or twenty years ago, the proportion of boys learning the business was much greater. They were generally apprenticed to the proprietors of the establishment, who employed one of the workmen to teach the boy, and usually allowing the teacher, for his trouble, all the advantage to be derived from his labour for the first four years, they claiming that advantage for the last three years of the boys apprenticeship. The materials used in the business being more costly than in most other manufacturing pursuits, and the loss from inexperienced hands occasionally considerable, the masters thought they were entitled to the services of the last three years. On the other hand, a journeyman did not like to run the risk of a boy's health for so long a period as seven years; hence the above regulations were adopted as the best, and fair to all parties. The boys were put to work, generally, at from thirteen to fourteen years of age. Since the establishment of the trades' unions, a master is not permitted to take an apprentice upon any terms.*

* A journeyman often pays to the master from ten to twenty pounds, or one shilling per week, on taking an apprentice, in consequence of the loss necessarily incurred by his inexperience.

5 What is the average of wages, in time of good trade, in the several branches?

The earnings of the men vary very much, in proportion to their skill,—from 18s. or 20s. to 25, 28, 30, 38, 42s. per week, and some, indeed, will earn considerably more. Women will earn from 8s. to 15s. per week,—one with an apprentice to whom she pays 2s. 6d per week, will often get from 20s. to 24s.

6. Do you observe any relation between the capability of earning great wages, and sobriety and intelligence?

Yes, generally.

7. Are the families of those who earn great wages more comfortable and better educated than those whose wages are only moderate?

Yes, generally.

8. What proportion of the workmen in the several branches can neither read nor write?

In the manufactory above alluded to, there are probably not half a dozen who cannot do both.

9. Do you observe that the workmen, in those branches or departments which require great ingenuity and skill, are superior in information and conduct to those whose labour is rather physical than mental? Which of these two classes of workmen receive the highest wages?

Those whose employment requires the greater " ingenuity and skill," are generally superior in intelligence and general conduct, which may be partly accounted for *by their being oftener in communication with the masters. Generally, too, they receive higher wages.*

10. Are the workmen in the several branches in separate unions?

Yes; stampers and braziers have each separate unions.

11. Do the unions regulate the prices only, or do they dictate to masters what men they shall employ?

They maintain a general control over the prices of work, but patterns and modes of working being different in different manufactories, it cannot be so positive and exact as in some other trades, such as the file and table knife trade, and many others. No one is allowed to work in what is called a regular manufactory, unless he have conformed to all the regulations of the union, and paid up his contributions.

12. Are the restrictive laws of the unions in full force in time of bad trade, or are they effective only when the demand for hands is great ?

The restrictions of the silversmiths' unions are pretty equally effective in good and bad trade; the unions are rich, and should any master resist their dictation, they can afford a handsome allowance weekly, equal to the previous earnings, to such workmen as lose their situations in consequence of an attempt to reduce wages. Workmen are sometimes unemployed for many months on this ground.

13. Have you been often inconvenienced in the execution of your orders, by the combination of workmen?

The inconvenience to masters in this trade may be described as being general and continuous, the unions much increasing the independence of the' men *as a body;* and restricting the liberty of the masters, as well as of individual workmen, though, probably not in so great a degree as in some other trades; partly on account of the work being so various, and as well as from the artisans being better informed than in most other branches of manufactures, hence they are much more reasonable.

The number of workmen in this branch is a little above four hundred. Independently of the handsome provision which the union secures to those out of employment, there is also a provision for the sick, with which the union is not at all connected. It is not a Friendly Society which affords so much weekly, but which gives at once to the claimant six pounds. None are admitted members until they have been three years in the business, and none after twenty-five years of age. The entrance fee is 8d. The funds are raised by collections in all the factories of this particular trade, each member contributing 6d. The claimant must have been sick and incapable of working for three successive months before he becomes entitled to this donation, and not even then, if he receive parochial relief. All this is excellent, and shows a manly independent spirit in the designers of these regulations. It would be well if other branches would imitate such conduct.

A member can make a second claim, if he have stood sound for twelve months, or having been sick for six successive months. Besides this provision for sickness, the sum of eight pounds, on the death of a member, is paid to the widow, provided he have not made a first claim. All such institutions are admirable, and deserve patronage and support. They are efforts of the artisan, to secure his own independence, instead of falling on the parish in time of necessity.

In those branches of manufacture in which there are no such provisions, the workmen frequently suffer the greatest possible distress. Families become .destitute, and are entirely dependent on parochial relief. The artisan should be taught to shun such dependence, as if fraught with infection. It leaves effects which scarcely any subsequent prosperity removes.

It is stated in answer to the thirteenth question, that the inconvenience felt by masters, in the plated manufacture, from the union regulating the wages of labour, has been much less than in many other branches of trade, in consequence of the greater intelligence of the workmen. This is indeed true. Some of the unions have been exceedingly intolerant and oppressive, and by their violence have materially injured their cause. The manner in which the unions are conducted, is a just criterion of the intelligence of the artisans associated. The tyranny, which has been exercised by several, has been despotic and reckless in the extreme, and the means employed to enforce the obedience of refractory or independent workmen, in the last degree violent and illegitimate, and unless corrected will inevitably be destructive of their own interests.

If they presume to have a right to protect labour, which is to them unquestionably capital and existence, reason, argument and liberality must be their weapons. To coerce, in the worst spirit of despotism, is to forfeit all claim to kindly consideration and sympathy. The subject of combinations is indeed worthy of study, and it is impossible, in an investigation like the present, to avoid a frequent allusion to it, in reference to the influence of such associations on the condition generally of the workmen. If they can be shown to secure a fair remuneration for labour—to diminish fluctuations in its demand—to promote self-respect and independence, and to lead to the cultivation of a better tone of mind, it will scarcely be doubted, that these are advantages which must be set against alleged and admitted evils.

The foregoing facts exhibit a favourable and just view of the mental and physical condition of an important class of workmen, and will be found to form a painful contrast with the circumstances of artisans in many other branches of trade. The causes of this superiority are imagined to be explicable under the following heads; but whatever opinion may be entertained on this subject, it will not be denied that the particular causes exist, and will necessarily exert considerable influence on the condition of those engaged in the manufacture.

1. The regulations of the trade unquestionably tend to keep the supply of labour within certain bounds, hence

they are generally denounced as despotic, and injurious to
the natural progress of the manufacture. That they may,
occasionally, in this point of view, be detrimental, will at
once be admitted; but the consideration is, whether the
evil preponderates over the good, not only in relation to
the artisan, but his employer. What permanently benefits
the former, may possibly be shown to be equally conducive
to the interests of the latter. It is not the advantage of
either to increase, beyond a legitimate demand, the productive power. Increased facilities in the ability to create,
never fail to augment the competition and to diminish
the profits of manufacturers.

An inordinate demand arising from excited and temporary
causes, would, were there no regulations limiting the introduction of hands, immediately bring into play additional
capital and establish a rate of production in harmony with
the fitful occasions. The power to meet such demands
invariably leads to the overstepping of it, and brings into
existence the numerous evils inseparable from the excess
of production. Were this power endowed with elasticity,
in virtue of which it could return within narrow limits,
after the cessation of the causes by which it had been
extended, the exercise of it would be harmless. But unfortunately it possesses no such property. Additional
factories are erected from the stimulus of the demand, so
that capital becomes invested in costly buildings, which
are profitable only in a period of commercial prosperity:
hands are, also, multiplied in accordance with the temporary
impulse imparted, and while these changes are regarded,
by the superficial observer, as the indications of a healthy
state of things—advantageous to all parties, new manufacturers spring up, possessing capital and enterprise, and

fiercely compete for a share of this demand, and then mark the results. The manufacturers having too large a capital invested in trade to be inactive, the struggle of competition commences, which leads to the diminution of profits; and by its tendency to keep production beyond demand creates a series of evils—reduced wages, increased bodily labour, partial employment, and, at last, an easy transition to the parish.

2. Another circumstance which is of advantage to the artisans in this particular occupation, is the limited number of manufacturers. When workmen can readily become masters, which unfortunately is the case in many of the branches of trade, either from the fewness or simplicity of the tools required, wages are always low, and the prevailing condition of the artisans is correspondingly degraded. The expensive nature of the articles employed in this manufacture, both in the materials and the tools used, renders it exceedingly difficult for individuals to change their position and become masters. This circumstance conduces, in an important degree, to the superiority of the silver-plated branch, in regard to the education, conduct and pecuniary circumstances of the workmen.

3. In many branches of trade children may be employed very young, but in this it is scarcely possible, hence they are seldom put to work much under fourteen years of age. The admitted respectability of the silver-plated manufacture, the rate of remuneration which it yields, conjoined with the difficulties of entering it, secure youths generally of some education, so that, with few exceptions, all the workmen can either read or write, in the majority of cases can do both.

M

4. The workmen, with few exceptions, are in large establishments, they are not, however, under special surveillance, as the artisans in cotton factories, who are indeed a necessary part of the complicated machinery in operation. Each individual is mostly employed by what is technically called "*piece*," that is, he is paid according to the amount or value of the work executed, and not according to time. The negligence or misconduct of one, does not generally interfere with the labours of another; occasionally, such is the case. The articles in their different stages of progress pass through various hands, consequently if interrupted in one stage, some inconvenience will probably be experienced by those to whom the further advancement of them belongs. The absence or negligence of one class of workmen, viz. the stampers, whose business it is to prepare the articles for many subsequent processes, frequently causes serious interruptions.

The advantages of a large establishment, that is where the artisan is employed on the premises of the master, are great, in a moral point of view, from the beneficial influence of example. The industrious and well regulated habits of the many, restrain the irregular and intemperate conduct of the few, or at least control the tendency to dissipation. There is no manufactory in which there is greater order, regularity, or sobriety than in the silver and plated ware branch. We have no hesitation in stating, that one of the circumstances which is particularly unfavourable to the progressive improvement of the artisans in this town, is, the facility they possess of working either at their own homes, or in small workshops or rooms rented by them, in which different branches of trade are often carried on. This perfect freedom from all restraint or superintendence, or the influence of regulations, either expressed or implied, tending to produce a general conformity of conduct, is the source of idleness and dissipation. The artisan in this case, works when it suits him, and too often plays and drinks when he ought to be otherwise employed. We have observed the most striking difference in the appearance and condition of individuals, in the same branch of trade, according to the degree of independence they possess in regard to this circumstance.

5. The workmen are not liable to be thrown out of employment by ingenious inventions or the application of machinery. No contrivance, however admirable, can dispense with the necessity of manual labour in this branch. The articles are intricate, difficult of execution, and ever changing in their designs. That which is excellent and the prevailing fashion of to-day, is modified by the taste or caprice of to-morrow. Each article is usually composed of many parts, and passes through very dissimilar processes of labour requiring different kinds and degrees of skill.

The important improvements which machinery has effected in several branches of manufactures, in various parts of the kingdom, have, at least, temporarily, greatly deteriorated the condition of the operatives. They have been either entirely thrown out of employment, or wages have been so seriously reduced, that their command of the common necessaries of life has been miserably abridged. It is indeed painful to observe, that where manufacturing improvements have been the most marked, and where the largest fortunes in the shortest period have been accumulated, the degradation and distress of the operatives have been proportionately aggravated. These remarks

M 2

are not made for the purpose of prejudicing the vulgar mind against such improvements, the facts have a value, however, in relation to the present inquiry which cannot be overlooked. The workmen, in the branch under consideration, are not liable to depression and fluctuations from such causes, by which manual labour is cheapened or superseded, hence a more permanently healthy condition of the trade would be anticipated.

The peculiar effects of these rapid improvéments are perceived not only in the condition of the artisans, but in the character of the manufacturers. Men spring up suddenly into a commanding position in society, with immense energies and determined enterprise—stimulated by one feeling—the thirst to make a fortune. The success of their exertions is in no degree retarded by any refined or delicate considerations concerning the mode—education gives no relish to participate in the pleasures of social life, time is too valuable to be wasted in the interchange of thought, or in the discussion of matters which have not an immediate and obvious practical application. No field opens to seduce the intellect to look abroad, or to impart the first elements of taste, by which the mind might be tempted to forget its rigid duty—which is action, and not contemplation. Thus, fortunes so created are too generally associated with little that is generous in sentiment, liberal in principle or elevated in view. The manufacturer is an animated machine, and as regular in the routine of his operations, and often as insensible of the condition and necessities of the artisans. The success which results, engenders an intolerant and overbearing disposition. The individual claims for wealth what belongs to mind, and looks upon all acquirements as things of no use in this world, unless they throw light on the process of money-making, the secret of which depends not on large cultivated mental powers, but on determined energy, and the concentration of a few faculties. A comprehensive and educated understanding, would throw obstacles in the way : it would suggest considerations interfering with the operations of tact, shrewdness and cunning. We have previously remarked, that the manufactures of this town, do not allow of the rapid accumulation of immense masses of wealth, hence the evils to which we allude, exist here in a modified degree compared with many other places. The slow creation of riches is accompanied with the gradual refinement and enlargement of the understanding, and the duties which an improved position imposes, are not forgotten in the one absorbing feeling of self.

We have endeavoured to explain the circumstances which appear to exert an important influence on the condition of the workmen in this particular manufacture ; and to which the better education and the higher morality of them, as well as their greater command of the necessaries of life, than is found in connexion with most other branches, must be ascribed. It has not been our business to consider the principles regulating the production of national wealth, but circumstances affecting individual happiness ; but while concentrating the attention on the latter, it is possible that views may have been presented bearing on the elucidation of the former.

The workmen in the silver-plated trade were not always as favourably circumstanced as at present. At one time, they were liable to great vicissitudes and severe distress, arising from an extraordinary increase in the hands employed. The fact is interesting and important to record. At the period to which we allude, the masters were allowed to take any number of apprentices, and to such an extent was this carried—far beyond the regular necessities of the manufacture—that on the occurrence of a slight depression many individuals were at once thrown out of employment, and others had only partial work. The artisans perceived the cause and endeavoured to correct it, by limiting the introduction of boys according to the natural extension of the trade, and to this is to be attributed, the steadiness of the scale of remuneration, the more regular employment, and the respectable position which they occupy as operatives.

In the examination of the silver and silver-plated manufacture, we have entered much more into details than space will allow with respect to other branches of trade. We have been thus particular, from the importance of the manufacture in question, whether viewed in regard to the capital employed in it, or the general respectability of the workmen; and further, from a desire to show clearly the influence of a pursuit, in which skill, taste and intelligence are exercised, in conjunction with particular regulations on the conduct and character of the artisans. Further illustrations of this influence, and not less valuable than any that have been adduced, might be drawn from an examination of the returns of a *given* number of the operatives, of all trades, at different periods, dependent on parochial relief, imprisoned for debt, or sued in the Court of Requests, members of sick clubs, depositors in the Savings' Bank, or the degree of education possessed as tested by the ability to read or write, which afford the best evidence of the condition of any portion of the working classes, but the want of space precludes such analysis.

Some of the returns, but not the comparisons to which we allude, are given in several parts of this inquiry.

This occupation is not particularly detrimental to health, at the same time it cannot be regarded as conducive to longevity. Several departments require close application both of the mind and body, but are accompanied with too little vigorous muscular exercise to counteract the effects of such application, and of an atmosphere which is often exceedingly impure, on the animal system.* There are departments, however, in which the labour is severe. The appearance of the workmen is not usually that of robust health; they are generally pallid or sallow in complexion, and suffer from the various forms of dyspepsia. In whatever relation they are studied, they present indeed a striking contrast to the workmen generally in this town, except the class which we next bring under consideration.

In order to arrive at a generally correct idea of the influence of this manufacture on health, we ascertained the number of individuals who died within a given time, and the ages at death, and the following are the calculations founded on the facts obtained.

* Many of the workshops are extremely unhealthy from the rooms being low, and especially from the burning of large gas-lights, by which the atmosphere is greatly deteriorated. The latter circumstance, we are convinced, is much more detrimental to health than is generally imagined.

Mean ages attained by persons dying above given ages in the Silversmiths' Benefit Society, as deduced from the mortality of the past twelve years.

Given age.	Age attained.
20	46.15
25	49.63
30	52.95
35	56.11
40	59.12
45	61.97
50	64.66
60	67.20
65	69.58
70	71.81
75	73.88

The value of life among the silversmiths is less than we had previously imagined. Indeed it is only a few degrees higher than that of the working classes generally in manufacturing towns. In Manchester, Leeds, and Liverpool, individuals in these classes, dying above 40, attain on an average the age of 58.97; in rural districts, 68.76. The advantage in favour of the silversmiths is so slight, that it scarcely deserves particular notice.

CHAPTER XII.

SAW MANUFACTURE.

The workmen in this branch of trade are, perhaps, in no degree inferior in intelligence, sobriety and general good conduct to those in the manufacture of which we have just treated. They have both equally their respective unions, which regulate wages, the introduction of apprentices and which, in time of sickness, afford a weekly allowance. The following answers to the subjoined questions will convey a correct idea of the condition of the artisans.

1. What are the principal branches of the saw-making department?

The saw trade is divided into three branches—saw-making, saw-handle making, and saw-grinding.

2. What parts are usually executed by boys or women?

Boys in the saw-making branch attend first to toothing and filing. Women are employed to rub and scour saws, and, also, to oil and wrap them up.

3. What number of workmen is there in the different branches?

In the saw-making branch, there are two hundred and eight journeymen,—about twenty of them not in union.

4. What number of boys or apprentices?

The number of boys is about one hundred and thirty, which exceeds what is allowed by the rules of the trade.

5. What number of women?

There is one female to about every eight men.

6. Were girls or women much employed in the trade thirty or forty years ago?

Always as at present.

7. What are the rules regulating the admission of apprentices?

The master is allowed two apprentices to five journeymen. During the bad time of trade, this regulation has not been strictly attended to by the masters.

8. What is the average of the wages in the different branches, supposing an individual to labour eleven hours per day?

There is so great a difference in the work, and such diversity of talent in the workmen, that it is scarcely possible to give an average. The following statement is not far from the truth :—
The few who are *datal** earn from 24s. to 32s. per week. The *piece-work* varies very much in its kind. Some departments will allow a person to earn from 35s. to 45s. per week, whilst others restrict the earnings to between 28s. and 30s.—28s. is about the average of the wages.

9. Are the workmen usually by the piece or datal?

Both by the piece and datal, but generally by the piece.

10. What proportion of the adults can read?

Nineteen out of twenty.

11. What proportion can write?

Nearly nineteen out of twenty.

12. What proportion of boys can read or write?

We are not aware that there are any that cannot do both.

13. Are the different branches of the trade in the same or different unions? If in different unions, is each under a separate and independent management.

In different unions, and their management is quite independent of each other.

* *Datal* means paid by the day or week—*piece*, for the amount of work executed.

14. What changes have taken place in the prices since 1814?

The saw-making branch, for making the best article, receives about the same as in 1814; but there is twenty per cent. more work in the articles than in 1814.

15. What proportion of men are in sick clubs?

About nine-tenths.

16. What proportion in secret orders?

About one-sixth.

17. Are the men, in sickness, or when out of work, relieved from any fund belonging to each branch of this trade?

Workmen belonging to the saw-making branch, in case of sickness, or when out of employment, receive a weekly allowance; and in case of death, a certain sum is paid towards defraying the funeral expenses. During the past two years, this branch has paid about £2000, principally to workmen out of employment. It has been in union, and regularly organised above forty years.

18. What proportion of the workmen are depositors in the Savings' Bank?

From the depression of trade, during the last two years, we doubt whether any deposits remain in the Savings' Bank.*

19. Are the prices as strictly enforced, in time of bad trade, as in time of good?

We have had great difficulty in maintaining the prices, but have generally been successful.

SAW-HANDLE MAKERS.

1. What is the number of men employed in this department of trade?

The number of men employed is about 120.

2. What is the number of boys employed, and what are the rules regulating their admission?

The number of boys is about 100, and there is no particular rule regulating their admission.

* In 1840, it is shewn, at page 133, that there were 34.

3. What is the number of females employed?

Women are not employed in this department of trade.

4. Are the men *datal* or by the *piece?*

The men work always by the piece.

5. What is the average of the weekly wages, and when were the present prices fixed?

The average earnings, 26s. per week. The prices were fixed in 1821, but many men are working at prices lower than at that time?

6. Are the men in union?

The men are in union, but one very imperfectly formed and conducted.

7. What proportion of the men can read?

About eighty.

8. Are the apprentices the property of the masters or the journeymen?

With few exceptions, they are the property of the journeymen.

SAW-GRINDERS.

1. What is the number of men employed in this department of trade?

The number of men in this department of the saw trade is nearly one hundred and twenty.

2. What is the number of boys employed, and what are the rules regulating their admission?

The number of apprentices is about 90. No journeyman is allowed to have more than one apprentice, unless the apprentice be in his twentieth year.

3. Are the men datal or by the piece?

With few exceptions, the men work by the piece.

4. What is the average of the weekly wages?

The average earnings are from 40s. to 50s. per week, out of which sum the grinder pays wheel rent, and the cost of stones and other articles required in grinding.

5 Are the men in union?

The men, with the exception of about 12, are in a union which was formed in 1819.

6. What proportion of the men can read?

About one hundred.

In the consideration of the silver and silver-plated manufacture, several conditions are stated which appear to be favourable to the workmen—such as restrictions on the introduction of apprentices, and the difficulty, from the capital required, for journeymen to become masters. The same exist, but not to an equal extent, in the saw trade. This is more liable to fluctuations from the greater competition resulting from this circumstance, and likewise from the manufacture depending largely on foreign markets. The well-being and intelligence of workmen will always be most marked in those branches in which the demand is the most regular. Neither inordinate prosperity nor adversity is conducive to the improvement of the artisan.

Many of the facts in the foregoing answers redound greatly to the credit of the operatives. Not to be able to read and write, is the exception and not the rule. It is also stated, that nine-tenths are in sick-clubs, which is perhaps a greater proportion, with the exception of the silver-plated branch, than in any other in the town. In some of the occupations, the proportion is little more than one-half. Men who are insufficiently remunerated for their labour, yet liable to the frequent vicissitudes of trade, cannot be expected to be provident, nor have they generally either the means or the inclination to improve their minds.

The researches of Mr. Felkin into the condition of the workmen in Nottingham, during the depression of trade in 1837, afford some valuable facts on this subject, and are evidence of the vastly superior circumstances of the artisans employed in the manufactures of this town.

Out of 452 stocking makers, 91 only were in sick clubs; about one in five. In 498 lace makers, 128; rather more than one in four. Of the smiths, one in five. How different are these proportions from what are furnished by the saw trade! Were there no other facts, on which to form an estimate of the condition of the artisans in the latter, these would be sufficient to establish the comparative comfort of the one class, and the comparative misery and degradation of the other.

The saw-making branch may be regarded as generally healthy. It is an occupation in which considerable muscular exertion is required, and yet the labour is not so severe as to make an undue call upon the energies of the system. The men are mostly well formed and strong, and live to a fair average age, taking into consideration that the employment is entirely within doors. The saw-grinders are among the most powerful of the artisans, either in this or any other manufacturing town. A great part of the labour is heavy, but several circumstances concur to prevent this exhausting the vital powers. The wheels in which they work are mostly propelled by water, being placed upon the streams, in the exquisitely beautiful situations within a few miles of the town; consequently, the artisans are liable to numerous interruptions, either from too much or too little water. The frequency of these interruptions has led many of them, to add to this employment the cultivation of the soil.

They have frequently either small farms, or plots of ground for garden purposes. The wheels, moreover, are always well ventilated, in consequence of dilapidated windows and roofs, for they are proverbially in a bad condition. The workmen, also, generally live in the country, and the wages they receive, which is an important circumstance, enable them to command the substantial necessaries of life. The combination of these conditions, satisfactorily explains the strong muscular frames which they possess. Further, the branch does not admit of the employment of boys at a tender age or of delicate constitution, the articles being too heavy for either to hold with advantage. Saw grinding is also entirely done on a wet stone, and the position of the grinder, when at work, is standing, so that the lungs have free play, which is not the case in other branches of grinding.

The saw grinders are peculiarly liable to accidents, from the breaking of stones and from becoming entangled in the machinery. This arises from two circumstances, the largeness of the stones on which they work, as well as the great length and weight of many of the articles which they grind. The larger the stones, combined with the rate of motion, and the more liable they are to break; and it is manifest that a saw, five or six feet in length, is much less under the command of the grinder than a penknife; hence greater the chance of becoming entangled in the machinery. Of the 42 deceased, since 1821, of which we have returns, five were killed by the breaking of stones; and the following are a part of the accidents which have happened to 78 *living* members in union.

1. Lame nine months, from the breaking of a stone.
2. Lame six months;—drawn over the stone.
3. Arm broken, from being entangled in the machinery.

4. Skull severely fractured;—was incapable of work for nine months, and the individual has broken eleven stones.

5. Drawn over the stone;—severely hurt;—in bed nine months.

6. Severely hurt—confined two months;—has broken seven stones.

7. Hand cut;—confined one month.

8. Leg entangled in the machinery;—for twelve months unable to work.

9. Arm severely lacerated;—lame three months.

10. Lamed, from the stone breaking;—ill three months.

11. Hand lacerated;—incapacitated from work.

12. Hand lacerated;—lame two months,

13. Leg broken, and now a cripple.

In this branch, there are only four affected with the disease peculiar to grinders, and these cases are more likely to have arisen from exposure to wet a'   ·old, than from the inhalatio

CHAPTER XIII.

EDGE TOOL TRADE.

The edge tool manufacture is divided into three branches, the forgers, the grinders and the hardeners; and each is in a separate and independent union. In this trade, a large capital is employed, and the manufacturers are generally men of wealth, enterprise and respectability. The business cannot be carried on without considerable capital, arising from the cost of the raw material and the long credit which is often unavoidably given, a great proportion of the articles being exported. The following particulars refer to one branch only—the forgers.

1. What parts of the edge tool forging department are usually executed by boys?

Boys strike.*

2. What number of workmen are there in this branch?

200 foremen and 200 strikers.

3 What number of boys or apprentices?

About fifty boys and apprentices.

* The articles being too heavy for one man to fashion into the desired form upon the anvil, the maker has the assistance of another, and this person is called the striker.

4. What is the average of the wages, supposing an individual to work eleven hours per day?

Foreman and striker, average £2 16s. per week; foreman, £1 14s., striker, £1 2s.

Our authority, on this subject, remarks :—

" We have named £2 16s. as the average of the whole of the hearths that we have employed ; but it is much less than what might be earned, if the men were industrious. We have selected a few books of those who are moderately steady, and we find in these that the average is £3 5s., which gives to the foreman £1 19s., and to the striker, £1 6s. The forgers are much in the habit of contracting debts with their employers. The money borrowed is very rarely for the purpose of benefiting their families."

5. Are the workmen usually by the piece, or datal ?

Altogether by the piece.

6. What proportion of the adults can read and write ?

About one-fifth.

7. What proportion of the workmen are in sick clubs ?

About three-fourths.

8. What proportion in secret orders ?

About one in five.

9. Are the men, in sickness, or when out of work, relieved from any fund belonging to each branch of the trade ?

Both in sickness and when out of employment.

10. Are the prices as strictly enforced, in time of bad trade, as in time of good ?

They have been strictly enforced for three years, during which time trade has been bad.

The workmen in this branch are, perhaps, as well remunerated for their labour as any class of artisans. In time of good trade, the wages will allow a liberal sum for the necessaries and comforts of life, as well as a surplus of means sufficient to provide against future wants. The small proportion capable of reading and writing, indicates a low state of mental culture. They are generally a fine, healthy and vigorous class of men, but unfortunately are

irregular and dissipated in their habits. The circumstances in which they are placed, are not favourable for
intellectual improvement, nor for inducing sobriety, tem-
perance or economical considerations.

1. The foregoing department does not offer much play
for the mind, nor are its faculties exercised by it, as in
many other branches. It demands great physical power
and ordinary attention. It will always be found, that in
those occupations in which there is little room for ingenuity
and skill, but excessive calls on the muscular energies, the
.artisans will be comparatively low in the scale of intelligence and prone to sensual excesses. Such is the fault of
their position. Severe labour produces exhaustion, the
feeling of which leads to indulgence in those things which
either remove it, or exhilarate the spirits.

2. The workmen, when they please to apply themselves
closely, can earn great wages, and knowing their ability to
do so, they often spend in idleness and dissipation the
fore-part of the week.

3. They work either alone, or in company with a striker,
and have not the advantage of frequent interchange of
thought, or that social communication which is enjoyed
by the silversmiths, the saw-makers, and by other branches.
In a well-conducted manufactory, the example, the intelligence and good feeling of the thinking class of workmen,
exercise a beneficial influence on the whole. Violent tendencies and extreme opinions are softened and modified by
the temperate reasoning and juster views of the better
informed.

According to the facts which are here stated, high wages do not alone secure a corresponding degree of education, and, perhaps, it would be unreasonable to calculate on such result. It is only one condition conducive to so desirable an end. When a pursuit exercises rather the muscular than the mental powers, the demands made upon the former, are never favourable to the development of the latter. Indeed we have observed a marked difference in the *form* of the head in individuals whose occupations call into play, in different degrees, the mental faculties. We are not disposed to ascribe this to an original difference of conformation, but to the different degrees in which the mental powers are exercised. Nature will not allow, to any great extent, an expenditure of energy in two different directions. The vigorous muscular exercise of the body must always be at the expense of the intellectual faculties. The supply which is necessary to support the body in constant and severe labour, leaves only a limited stream of blood and nervous energy to stimulate and feed the anterior region of the brain. Hence in the forgers, and in all persons similarly circumstanced in the trades in this town, we perceive a large development of the head posteriorly and laterally. The forehead is usually low and retreating, and the space between the crown of the head and the ears exhibits a very limited expansion. On the contrary, in artisans whose business exercises the thinking faculties in a greater degree than the muscles, the head gains in height and development both in the anterior and lateral portions of it.

CHAPTER XIV.

SPRING KNIFE MANUFACTURE.

The condition of this branch of trade affords a striking contrast, in all respects, to the branches previously considered. The workmen are among the worst paid in the town, and in a period of commercial depression, suffer much more severely than any other class, both in the reduction of prices and the want of employment. In the better or finer articles, some may earn 30s. per week, but in general the wages are excessively low. Before we proceed to explain the causes, we present the following facts, which are necessary to enable the reader to judge of the correctness of our reasoning.

1. What parts of the spring knife manufacture are executed by boys?

Boys nine or ten years of age may be made useful in this branch, but are seldom intrusted to make even inferior articles before the age of thirteen or fourteen.

2. What is the number of workmen in this branch?

Spring knife hafters, about	1400
Scale and spring forgers	150
Blade forgers	300
Pocket blade grinders	100
Pen blade grinders	300
	2250

Apprentices, (about 600,) and other workmen, not included under the above heads, make the number about 3000.

3. What are the rules regulating the introduction of apprentices?

There are no rules, the trade is open.

4. What is the average of wages in this branch?

The average of wages varies considerably. A few superior workmen may earn from 30s. to 40s. per week. In the first manufactories of the town, the average is from 16s. to 25s. But in many of the inferior manufactories, the workmen are receiving no more than 12s. or 16s.*

5. Are the workmen usually by the piece?

Almost entirely.

6. What proportion of the adults can read?

Not above one-half, and not one-fourth moderately well.

7. What proportion can write?

About one-fifth.

8. What proportion of the boys can read and write?

About three-fifths can read. One-fourth can write?

9. Is this branch in union? No.

10. What proportion of the adults is in sick clubs?

The question is difficult to answer. Perhaps two-thirds.

11. What proportion in secret orders? One-tenth.

12. Are the workmen, in sickness, or when out of employment, relieved from any fund belonging to the trade?

This was the case formerly, *when the trade was in union*, but is not now.

13. What proportion of the workmen are depositors in the Savings' Bank.

Not more than one-fifth.

14. What proportion of the men marry under twenty-four years of age?

Two out of every three. Many before twenty.

15. At what age are boys usually put to work?

Great numbers from eight to nine years of age.

From these facts, it is obvious, that the workmen in this particular branch are much less favourably circumstanced than the saw-makers or the silversmiths. Their condition, in periods of commercial distress, is indeed deplorable.

* At the present time, June 1843, this scale of wages is very greatly reduced.

They have no resources on which to fall back, hence the moment the demand for labour fails, they are compelled to apply for parochial relief, or what is exceedingly detrimental to their interests, *to manufacture on their own account, and sell what they produce at miserably low prices.* The causes of their peculiar and unfortunate position may be thus briefly explained :—

1. The first and most important to bring under consideration, is the very small capital which is required to manufacture articles of cutlery. The tools of the forger, hafter or putter together, are few, simple and easily procured. A few pounds will enable the cutler to commence operations, and those parts which it is not his business to execute, are performed by others, whose co-operation is always readily obtained when such necessity exists. The want of employment is felt equally by all engaged in the branch, from the forger of the blade to the grinder. Necessity is thus constantly converting workmen into petty masters, who not only sink the profit of the manufacturer, but even sacrifice a large proportion of the ordinary wages of labour. Their goods are purchased by the merchants, and a numerous class of individuals, who have only recently sprung into existence,—hardware dealers, who travel the country, selling them by public auction, or dispose of them in immense quantities to hawkers and small shopkeepers. It is important to point out this class of individuals, but charity forbids that we should do more than name them. The ease with which workmen become manufacturers is the great curse of this branch.

2. From what is here stated, it would scarcely be imagined possible for the workmen to be in union. There is one circumstance indispensably necessary to enable

them in any branch to form and maintain one ;—*that is, the difficulty of the transition from journeymen to masters.* Without this circumstance to aid the artisans, the attempt may be made, but it scarcely can be successful. The frequent necessities of the workmen, during even a slight depression of trade, would defeat any such intention, and experience has established the fact.

3. Another disadvantage under which this branch labours, is the facility which it offers for the employment of children at an early age. Many of the operations may be performed by them ; hence, there is an inducement superadded to the necessities of the parents, to put them early to work. This, indeed, is a great evil. It strikes at the root of all improvement. It is keeping up a continuous stream of poor and uneducated workmen. In times of commercial prosperity, there is at once an influx of productive labour into the manufacture, quite equal to any temporary or fitful demand. It will, therefore, readily be imagined, that on the occurrence of depression, many hands will be thrown out of employment, which is the case. The productive power is usually far in advance of the regular demand. These three causes are amply sufficient to account for the unfavourable condition of the artisans, and that such causes have long been in operation, is manifest from the small proportion able to read and write, the numbers who are neither in sick clubs nor secret orders, and the early age at which many marry. These facts are evidence of a low and degraded condition. The worse paid the workmen in any branch, or in other words, the less capable they are of maintaining a family, *the earlier do they always marry.* Poverty, from the absence of intelligence and a healthy tone of mind, is prone to aggravate and multiply its evils.

CHAPTER XV.

FILE TRADE.

This manufacture differs in several important respects from the branches previously considered, hence the investigation of it will suggest a few remarks not altogether uninstructive. It will, however, be confined principally to one department of the trade, viz., the file-cutters. The manufactures which have already been brought under notice, have been selected from the illustrations which they afford of the influence of certain conditions and regulations on the circumstances of the working classes in this district.

1. What are the different branches in the file trade?

Four, viz., forgers, grinders, cutters and hardeners. The cutters and forgers are in one union. The grinders and hardeners are in seperate unions. Our remarks are confined to the two first branches.

2. What parts are usually executed by boys or women?

Boys and women are employed in file-cutting.

3. What number of workmen are there in the different branches?

Forgers, 360; strikers, who assist the forgers, 160; Cutters, 900.

4. What number of boys or apprentices?

Boys, seven hundred.

5. What number of women?

One hundred. Total, 2220, leaving out of consideration the grinders and hardeners.

6. Were girls or women much employed in the trade thirty or forty years ago.

Not to one-third the extent as at present.

7. What are the rules regulating the admission of apprentices?

A master is allowed to take two apprentices; if there be several in the firm, two each. A journeyman until he be twenty-five years of age, is not allowed to take an apprentice; nor a second, not even his own son, unless the first apprentice be in his last year.

8. What is the average of wages in the different branches, supposing an individual to labour eleven hours per day?

FORGERS.

	£	s.	d.			£	s.	d.
Double hand hearths, average,	2	19	7	{	Foreman	1	12	10
Single hand hearths	1	11	10	{	Striker...	1	6	9
Saw file hearths	1	3	7					

FILE-CUTTERS.

	£	s.	d.
A man...average,	1	2	6
A man and boy	1	11	8
A man and two boys.....	2	0	6
By reference to thirty books of file-cutters, men of *steady* habits, each having the assistance of a boy, the average per week was found to be	1	18	6
A grinder ....average,	1	14	0
A grinder and boy	2	7	4

The average wages of the hardeners, who are employed by time, is 24s. per week; in general they have an opportunity of making over time, and 27s. per week may be regarded as a fair average.

The wages of women, employed to scour and clean the files, are 9s. per week.

REMARKS.

DOUBLE HAND FORGERS.*—In examining our books, the highest average of one hearth is found to be £4 17s. per week, and the

---

* In which a maker and striker are employed.

lowest £1 10s. Single hand forgers, highest £1 14s. 9d., lowest £1 10s. Saw file forgers, highest 18s., lowest, 14s. These differences arise from various causes: some men are more skilful and industrious than others, and one kind of work affords a better remuneration than another. *The main causes are the more or less industrious habits of the artisan.*

9. Are the workmen usually by the piece, or datal?

Entirely by the piece.

10. What proportion of the adults can read?

About eighty per cent.

11. What proportion can write?

Seventy per cent.

12. What proportion of boys can read or write?

Between 80 and 90 per cent. can read; 75 per cent. can write.

13. What proportion of the men is in sick clubs?

80 per cent.

14. What proportion in secret orders?

25 per cent.

15. Are the men in sickness, or when out of work, relieved from any fund belonging to each branch of this trade?

There is nothing allowed by the union. There is a weekly collection in the factory towards the support of the sick. In case of death, the union pays two pounds. On the death of the wife, or son employed in the trade, one pound.

16. What proportion of the workmen are depositors in the Savings' Bank?

A very small number.

17. Are the prices as strictly enforced in time of bad trade as in time of good?

This was not the case formerly, but is now, from the workmen being firmly united.

From these facts it would appear, that the condition of the file-cutters is not equal to that of the silversmiths or saw-makers. We observe a smaller proportion capable of reading or writing, as well as being members of sick societies and of secret orders. The union by which they are governed, has always been maintained with much greater difficulty than in either of the other two manufactures. In circumstances, they may be regarded as intermediate between the silversmiths and the spring-knife cutlers. They do not enjoy the comfort and independence of the former, nor are they subject to the misery or occasional distress of the latter. The causes of their peculiar situation are the following.

1. The admission of apprentices is not opposed by the same difficulties as in the silver-plated ware and saw-manufactures. In evidence of this, the apprentices and women are nearly equal in number to the journeymen; hence there is manifestly a growing tendency in the branch to increase beyond the ratio of a regular demand. When trade is exceedingly good for several years, new masters spring up and the journeymen are anxious to take apprentices, thus rapidly multiplying the productive power. This has clearly been the case in the file-cutting department, as is shown by the great number of apprentices. It is stated in the foregoing pages, that in a highly respectable silver and plated ware manufactory, the proportion of boys was nine to fifty-six men, which is about the average in the trade generally. Suppose the demands for labour to be in both branches equally urgent, and to continue for the same length of time, how very different would be the amount of increase in the productive powers in each!

Commercial prosperity is always temporary, seldom continuing beyond four or five consecutive years; and the depression which follows, bears a strict relation to the degree of prosperity by which it has been preceded. The more palmy or intoxicating its character, the more prolonged and severe is the misery. The file-cutters, it has been remarked, have had great difficulty in maintaining their union, and have occasionally failed. No branch can permanently maintain one, *that admits of a large increase in the amount of its productive power.* The want of trade throws too great a number out of employment, to be relieved or assisted by those who have full or only partial work, consequently, necessity compels the needy or starving to accept employment almost on any terms. A few months ago, there were 118 file-cutters alone on the parish, from which may be inferred the generally prevailing distress of the branch. Of the silversmiths, at the same time, there were only 14, and of the saw-makers the same number. Of the 200 cases taken indiscriminately from the books of the parish surgeons, in order to ascertain the nature of the prevailing diseases and the occupations of the individuals, 23, or about one-ninth are the cases of persons in the file trade. Of the silversmiths we have only four, and of the saw and saw-handle makers six. Allowing for the difference in the numerical strength of these branches, a much greater degree of misery evidently exists in the file trade than in the others. When so great a proportion, out of a given number is sick and dependent on the parish, it is not unjust to infer, that the artisans generally in this branch are in an exceedingly depressed condition.

2. Another important difference between this and the silver-plated branch, is the much earlier age at which boys can be employed in the former. The dissipation, idleness or necessity of parents, causes them to put their children to work, years before they ought to leave school, so that the addition made to the branch, is not from the educated of the rising generation, but from a class which have scarcely received any instruction at all. So long as this

principle is acted upon, it will be in vain for the workmen to attempt to better materially their condition. All their improvements must spring from knowledge. Were it a rule that none should be admitted into the trade before thirteen years of age, and not even then, unless they could read and write, it would effect a more salutary change in the moral, social and physical condition of this class of artisans than any other scheme that can be contemplated.

CHAPTER XVI.

FORK GRINDERS.

———

In addition to the trades which have already been brought under consideration, we shall adduce one more, as the analysis of it will present a vivid but painful picture of the condition of an extensive class of artisans in this town. The branch we shall select, viz., the fork grinders, is perhaps more destructive to human life than any pursuit in the united empire . It exceeds, however, only in a few degrees many other branches of grinding, as subsequent facts will show. In the foregoing pages we have mentioned, the saw-grinders, who are unquestionably for health and vigour of constitution, and for their command of the necessaries of life, superior to any large class of artisans in the town. Their employment renders them liable to frequent accidents, but the wet stone being invariably used, there is nothing injurious to life except what universally belongs to laborious occupations. The wet grinding is generally confined to saws, scythes and edge-tools; the dry to an extensive class of small articles, such as razors, scissors, pen and pocket knives, forks, needles, &c. The wet stone is also partially used in the grinding of some of these articles. The more destructive the nature of these branches, and the lower is the rate of wages and the more precarious is employment. The ignorance of the artisans is somewhat proportionate to the baneful tendency of the pursuit, and it is this ignorance and its necessarily associated evils,— dissipation, idleness and immorality, which account for what otherwise would be a paradox, that the remuneration and the steadiness of employment diminish in the ratio of the increase in the aggravated tendency of the occupation. This conclusion is deduced from elaborate investigations into various branches of manufacture. The want of space will permit us to treat only, on this occasion of fork-grinding.

We will briefly explain the nature of this branch. Forks are either forged or cast. By the former process, they are hammered into the required form ; by the latter, the metal in a liquid state runs into moulds having the impression of the article, and thus it is at once fashioned. The forged fork is durable and useful. The cast fork, is brittle and useless, and may be regarded as a gross imposition upon the purchaser. The former is often made of the best steel ; the latter of the basest metal. It is computed by good authorities, that about half the forks are cast, hence some idea may be formed of the roguery which is practised upon the public, for indeed it deserves no milder term. The next step in the manufacture, is grinding, and this is performed always on a *dry* stone. Several articles of cutlery are in the first place ground on a dry stone, and afterwards on a wet one. The former is a more expeditious operation than the latter, as will readily be conceived. Fork-grinding is always performed on a dry stone, and in this consists the peculiarly destructive character of the branch. In the room in which it is carried on there are generally from eight to ten individuals at work, and the dust which is created, composed of the fine particles of stone and metal, rises in clouds and pervades the atmosphere to which they are confined.

The dust which is thus every moment inhaled, gradually undermines the vigour of the constitution, and produces permanent disease of the lungs, accompanied by difficulty of breathing, cough, and a wasting of the animal frame, often at the early age of twenty-five. Such is the destructive tendency of the occupation, that grinders in other departments frequently refuse to work in the same room, and many sick clubs have an especial rule against the admission of dry grinders generally, as they would draw largely on the funds from frequent and long continued sickness. We will proceed to analyse the following facts, bearing on the condition of this particular branch.

The Men employed			97
The Boys ditto			100
The number of men	from 21 to 25 years of age		28
do. do.	from 25 to 30	do.	28
do. do.	from 30 to 35	do.	8
do. do.	from 35 to 40	do.	14
do. do.	from 40 and upwards		19
		Total	97
The number of boys	from 10 to 15 years of age		39
do. do.	from 15 to 20	do.	51
do. do	from 20 to 21	do.	10
		Total	100

Among the 19 men above 40 years of age, there are only three who have attained 50 years; and it is remarkable

o

that ten of the 19 either commenced this kind of work late in life, or passed several years in the army, as the following particulars show :—

    A. 64 years of age, was 25 when he began the trade.
    B. 54   do.   was 30   do.   do.
    C. 55   do.   was 26   do.   do.
    D. 50. Six years in the army.
    E. 48. Twenty-three years ditto.
    F. 50. Ten years out of the trade.
    G. 48. Twenty-four years out of the trade.
    H.   Unable to work, from lameness.
    I. 40. Ten years a gamekeeper.
    J.   Ten years out of the trade.

Deducting these ten from the 97 men, there are 56 under 30 years of age, eight from 30 to 35, fourteen from 35 to 40, nine above 40 and under 50 : and in the class from 35 to 40, there are some who have not worked regularly at the trade from youth. The numbers at these different ages, show the extraordinary mortality that must take place. What an immense proportion must die under 30 years of age! There are 56 under 30, and only eight from 30 to 35 ; consequently the greater part of the 56 die before attaining 30 years of age.

We have the names and ages of those who have died within stated periods,* hence unquestionable evidence of the rate of mortality. The number of workmen in the branch in 1820 was 80, and the deaths in the five following years were 20, and at these ages—

    * We have no account of the numbers that may have left the trade, or that die unconnected with the union of this particular branch, from one given period to another.

Six	24 years of age or under.
Six	30 ditto
Two	31 ditto
Three	34 ditto
One	40 ditto
One	50, entered the trade at 24 years of age.
One	50, twenty-three years in the army.

Thus, of the 20 deaths, 17 were of persons under 34 years of age. There are no records of the deaths of those under 21 years of age. · At that period one-fourth of the number employed died every five years—a rate of mortality exceeding every thing previously known in any branch of manufacture, or in any pursuit or occupation.. We have also the names and ages of 61 persons who died from 1825 to 1840, and we observe the same melancholy facts. Ages at which the 61 have died.

Four..................	22 years of age or under.
Five..................	24 ditto.
Thirteen	26 ditto.
Seven	28 ditto.
Six	30 ditto.
Nine..................	34 ditto.
Three	36 ditto.
Seven	38 ditto.
Three	40 ditto.
Three	46 ditto.
One	48 ditto.

Of the nine who attained the age of 34, one was ten years a sailor; the one 48 years of age was fifteen years in the army. Of the three 46 years of age, one was twelve years a soldier, and another commenced work at 23. Of the seven 38 years of age, one was ten years engaged in another pursuit.

o 2

According to these facts, 35 of the 61 died under 30 years of age; and under 36 years, 47. Of the remaining 14, above 36 years of age, four are to be deducted, either from having commenced the business late in life, or from having been withdrawn from the influence of it for a series of years. We do not hesitate to assert, that this is a picture of wretchedness, which has no parallel in the annals of any country, or in the records of any trade. But these figures will not convey to readers generally a correct idea of the extraordinary rate of mortality to which the workmen are subject, unless compared with the ratio of deaths at different periods, above twenty-one years of age, in this town and the country generally. It is only by such comparison, that just notions can be formed of the awful destruction of human life in this particular branch. The fork-grinders, in their recent admirable and temperate Address to the Public, in alluding to the baneful nature of the business, thus express themselves :—

" But, worthy townsmen, if these were the worst complaints we " could lay before you, we might have imposed upon ourselves the " hard duty of contentment. It is part of our duty to allude to " the destructive influence of our trade, which is a most serious " part of the question; for, be it known, that in respect to the per- " nicious effect of grinding trades upon health, our branch is by "far the worst. We can show, by irresistible facts, drawn from " the statistics of our trade, that the average age of fork-grinders .." does not exceed thirty years. Nor is this to be wondered at, " considering the poisonous atmosphere we have to breathe, which " renders the far greater part of us mere shadows of men, and " produces a complication of diseases, of which the most formidable " is the asthma and dry cough, known by the name of the grinders' " complaint, attended as it is by consumption, which no medical " man can cure. In such cases life is a burden to the poor suf- " ferers. Their frames are gradually emaciated and wasted by a " repetition of slow tortures; and when they have nearly closed " their mortal career, they have perhaps the bitter reflection of " leaving behind them, their wives and poor helpless infants to " suffer the horrors of want, unpitied or relieved by any."

This is no exaggerated picture of misery. The terms in which they express themselves are too mild for the evils under which they labour,—for the aggravated sufferings by which life is embittered. The analysis of these evils presents darker outlines of wretchedness than their own words pourtray. The following facts confirm the justness of these remarks.

Actual deaths, at particular ages in England and Wales, during 1838 and 1839 ; in Sheffield, from 1837 to 1841 ; and amongst the Fork-Grinders, from 1825 to 1840, above 20 Years of age.

	England and Wales.	Sheffield.	Fork Grinders.
20 to 29	26,289	685	29
30 to 39	22,349	611	25
40 to 49	20,752	589	7
50 to 59	20,797	579	0
At all Ages above 20.	163,905	3724	61

Comparison of deaths at certain ages, out of 1000 deaths above 20 years of age, in England and Wales.—Sheffield generally, and of the Fork-Grinders particularly.

	England and Wales. 1830–9	Sheffield generally. 1837–41.	Fork Grinders. 1825–40.
20 to 29	160	184	475
30 to 39	136	164	410
40 to 49	126	158	115
50 to 59	127	155	0
From 20 to 60	559	661	1000
At all Ages above 20.	1000	1000	1000

Thus in 1000 deaths of persons above 20 years of age, the proportion between 20 and 29 years, in England and Wales, is annually 160. In Sheffield, 184; but among the fork-grinders, the proportion is the appalling number 475; so that between these two periods, three in this trade die to one in the kingdom generally.

Between the ages of 30 and 39, a still greater disparity presents itself. In the Kingdom, 136 only in the 1000 die annually between these two periods. In Sheffield, 164; but in the fork-grinding branch, 410; so that between 20 and 40 years of age, in this trade, 885 perish out of the 1000; while in the kingdom at large, only 296. Another step in the analysis, and we perceive that between 40 and 49, in the kingdom, 126 die; in this town, 155; and in this branch, 115, which completes the 1000. They are all killed off. For in carrying forward the inquiry we observe that between 50 and 59, in the kingdom, 127 die; and in Sheffield, 155: but among the fork-grinders, there is not a single individual left. After this period of life, there are remaining in the kingdom, of the 1000, 441; and in the town, 339: but none in this branch of manufacture.

This high rate of mortality does not, however, mark the exact difference in the suffering of the parties compared. How various are the causes of death among mankind at every period of life! How great is the proportion swept away by acute diseases, in which there is neither much pain, nor protracted misery!

But this is not the case with the fork-grinders. The rate at which they perish, shows that they are not subject to the ordinary causes of death. The dust which they every moment inhale,—the poisonous atmosphere which they breathe, gradually destroys the functions of the lungs, rendering existence one continued series of distress, pain, and anxiety. The inability to work, and yet the necessity to labour, creates a degree of wretchedness and suffering easier to imagine than describe. But the wretchedness is not confined to the individual A wife and increasing family are involved in the accumulated evils. Poverty, yoked with disease, embitters and shortens life in a thousand forms, but all forms of misery. Can the finer feelings of the heart grow and expand in such a soil? Where the struggle is to support existence, and succeeds only by sacrifices and expedients from day to day, let us calculate rather on immoralities stepping into crimes of darker hue, than virtues invigorated by the ordeal of penury and pain. Virtues are like plants, they flourish best in a rich and well cultivated soil,—the popular virtues of mankind, which are rather exemptions from vice than active and spiritualized emotions, exhibiting in the every day occupations of life the charities which faint not, nor seek display.

A high rate of mortality might with considerable accuracy be inferred from the proportion of minors in the branch to the adults. This trade had in 1820, eighty adult workmen, and in 1841, ninety-seven; and yet it is evident, from the number and ages of the boys given, that, in the course of a few years there is an immense influx of hands into the branch—an influx not observed in the extension of it, *simply because they are killed off in a ratio somewhat proportionate to the increase.* If the workmen died only in the ratio of those in other branches, the numbers in this particular manufacture would be doubled every few years. Though the numbers are thus rapidly reduced, the proportion of minors to adults, is nevertheless too great to secure comfort and becoming independence to those engaged in it. The increase of hands exceeds the demands of the market, and, as a natural consequence, the workmen are unable to maintain steady and remunerative wages. No union or combination can be permanently supported under such circumstances. The misery which occurs in periods of commercial depression cannot be relieved by any existing funds, hence necessity dissolves the elements previously associated.

We have found, in inquiries into the state of the labouring classes in this town, that the proportion of the minors to adult workmen affords a generally correct measure of the physical, moral and intellectual condition of the latter. Greater the proportion, and the more miserable and dependent are the workmen—receiving low wages, subject to frequent vicissitudes, and never in a position to provide against the distresses of adverse seasons. Smaller the proportion, and greater is the command over the comforts and necessaries of life, and the less liable are the artisans to fluctuations in the demand for their labour. Among the best paid branches in this town and in perfect union, are the silver-plated and the edge-tool. In the former, the minors to the adults are 16 per cent. In the latter, 12½ per cent. In the worst paid, and not in combination, the spring-knife branch, the per centage is about 25, and the artisans are generally in a wretched state, save the few who are excellent hands, or fortunately in the employ of liberal and benevolent masters. The minors to adults in the fork-grinding department is 103 per cent., which, as we have already remarked, is too great for the permanent well being of the branch, though certainly the undue extension of it is in a great measure controlled by the high rate of mortality in it. The 103 per cent. is scarcely a greater proportion than the 25 per cent. in the spring-knife manufacture, in reference to the increase of the trade, because in the one, the workmen are *killed off* in a correspondingly greater ratio than in the other.

In confirmation of this fact, it is found, on examination, that among the ninety-seven men, about thirty at this moment are suffering, in various degrees, from the disease peculiar to this occupation, and which is known by the name—Grinders' Asthma. The disease is seated in the lungs and the air passages, and the progress of it is accompanied with the gradual disorganization of these important organs. In its advanced stages, it admits neither of cure nor of any material alleviation. In the early stages, the only efficient remedy is the withdrawal from the influence of the exciting cause; but how is this to be effected by men who depend from day to day upon their labour, and whose industry from early life has been confined to one particular branch? Here, then, is the melancholy truth that nearly one-third of this class of artisans, in addition to the poverty and wretchedness common to the whole, is in a state of actual disease—and disease which no art can cure. Fiction can add no colour or touches to a picture like this. Truth transcends the gaudy embellishments of imagination. The distempered fancy has here no room to exercise her powers.

Further evidence of the wretched state of the fork-grinders—and the remark applies with great truth to grinders generally—is the low state of education among

them. Of the 197 men and boys, 109 can read only, and
69 can write. Thus, in a Christian country—a country
that expends vast wealth in attempting to educate
and enlighten the dark heathen—one-half of an important
body of human beings, near this source of benevolence and
comprehensive charity, actually cannot read, and about
two-thirds cannot write! How great is the amount of
good that might be effected, if the benevolent would concentrate their exertions in the vicinity of their own threshold!

The fork-grinder, in common with all other grinders, is
subject to heavy and peculiar expenses. The artisan in
most branches has to pay neither for the tools which he
uses, nor the room which he occupies, but this is not the
case with the grinder. They form indeed a serious item
in his necessary expenditure. For the steam power
belonging to one trough, or which moves the stone at
which he works, the annual cost is eight guineas. If the
individual has an apprentice, an additional four guineas;
if two apprentices, the total annual charge is twenty guineas.
Besides these expenses, he has to defray the cost of the
stone and all its accompanying apparatus. In addition to
these charges, he has, in common with the more favoured
artisan, house rent and taxes. These are circumstances
which cannot be overlooked in this inquiry, exercising an
important influence on his condition. Commercial depression in his case, is fraught with severe hardships. He
cannot diminish his necessary or unavoidable expenses in
the ratio of his limited income, the consequence is that a
season of adversity, scarcity of employment and wages
miserably low, force him to make every possible sacrifice
to maintain his position,—to keep together his stock of
working tools. To effect this the little that he may have

saved is spent; his clothes and his furniture are either sold or pawned, and thus, by degrees, he sinks into the extreme of poverty and wretchedness, and from disease and a complication of evils passes through a process of tedious suffering into a premature grave.

The extensive researches in which we have long been engaged concerning the circumstances of the working classes of this town, have furnished numerous facts bearing especially on their physical and intellectual condition, and the influence of different occupations on health and longevity. The introduction of them, however, would trespass largely on our very limited space, and we must therefore content ourselves with stating simply some of the results at which we have arrived, respecting a class of individuals peculiarly and painfully situated, viz., the grinders. They have an urgent claim on our attention, and we trust that the evils under which they labour will at no distant period awaken that of the legislature. The following table exhibits the influence of the pursuit on the duration of life, in six branches, and the results are compared with the value of life in the town generally, in England and Wales, and in the Midland Counties. The comparisons will enable the reader to form a just idea of the awfully destructive tendency of grinding.

Mean ages attained by persons dying, above given ages, amongst several classes of Grinders in Sheffield and the neighbourhood; compared with the same facts in the Sheffield registration district generally, to which are, also, added, the same calculations as derived from the male mortality of England and Wales, and of the Midland Counties.*

Given age	Saw Grinders.	Scissor Grinders.	Razor Grinders.	Pen blade Grinders.	Needle Grinders.	Fork Grinders.	Sheffield Registration District.	England and Wales.	Midland Counties.
20	48.68	38 23	31.88	32.73	31.17	29.73	52.39	54.97	57.00
25	49.33	40 39	34.87	36.22	33.86	32.85	54.36	57.52	59.71
30	50.50	42.82	38.09	39.67	36.77	36.01	56.25	60.06	62.28
35	51.97	45.53	41.53	43.08	39.90	39.21	58.83	62.55	64.66
40	53.77	48.53	45.21	46.45	43.25	42.44	61.57	64.90	66.76
45	55.88	51.80	48.73	49.79	46.82	45.71	64,11	67.16	68.68
50	58.30	55.36	53.25	53.09	No	No	66.64	69.36	70.45
55	61.04	59.20	57.60	56.34	data.	data.	69.21	71.60	72 25
60	64.09	63.31	62.19	No	—	—	71.90	73.96	74.29
65	67.46	No	No	data.	—	—	74.80	76.49	76.58
70	71.15	data.	data.	—	—	—	77.93	79.26	79.24

This table exhibits the vast difference in the expectation of life in these branches, compared even with the population generally of the town, but especially with the two last columns. We have already stated the reasons why the artisans in the saw-grinding branch, in physical condition, are so superior to the rest of the class, and the difference appears in a very striking point of view in the comparisons which are here given. After forty-five years of age, we

* These counties, comprising the fifteenth Registration Division, are selected as being the nearest approach to a large agricultural district, to the exclusion from our comparison of the West-Riding of Yorkshire, which contains a great admixture of the manufacturing population. The fifteenth division extends over the counties of Derby, Leicester, Northampton, Nottingham and Rutland; also the Northern part of Lincolnshire. We have included no large manufacturing town except Nottingham, which is not so populous as to influence materially the results.

have no data in the needle and fork grinders; with the
exception of a few solitary individuals, they are killed off;
and in the other three branches, we soon cease to have any
facts to continue the comparison. It is somewhat singular,
however, that the mean age at death, of all who die above
eighty years of age, in England and Wales, is 85.53 years,
and in the whole parish of Sheffield, 85.83. This equality,
above eighty years of age, arises probably from this circumstance, that the few who attain to an advanced age in the
town must originally have possessed very vigorous constitutions, to have enabled them to resist the influences of
a manufacturing district.

CHAPTER XVII.

SICK CLUBS OR FRIENDLY SOCIETIES AND SECRET ORDERS.

———

The following tables give the number of clubs and secret orders in the town, and the ages and trades of the members in seven of the former. The inquiry was at first suggested by observing the frequent failure of benefit societies, which is known to be a common occurrence and fraught with severe hardships to the labouring classes. To point out the causes, it was necessary to be acquainted with the ages of the members, the amount of their monthly contributions, and the rate of relief when sick. It was found, however, impossible to acquire this information to the extent desired ; the clubs, with the exceptions here given, expressing a decided hostility to such investigations.

The insolvency of clubs, after they have existed for twenty or thirty-five years, is of frequent occurrence, by which men who have contributed to them, perhaps, during the whole of this time with little advantage, are deprived of relief, at a period of life when sickness and disease give them an urgent and just claim on the funds. Many such cases having fallen under our observation, during the exercise of professional duties, our attention was naturally awakened to the consideration of the causes of these frequently occurring evils. Had our investigations been met in a liberal spirit, much valuable information would have been attained on this important subject, clearly to the advantage of all such associations. The members generally have, however, insuperable prejudices against such researches.

The causes of insolvency are principally to be ascribed to too small a monthly contribution in aid of the funds, *and too large an amount given to the sick, or for a period on full pay longer than what is proper.* To demonstrate these facts it is only necessary to know the number of members, and to determine the average rate of sickness and of deaths. The monthly contribution to many of the clubs is a shilling or fifteen pence only; out of which sum three pence is usually spent in drink, or appropriated to general purposes. A member, when sick ordinarily receives 10s. per week for ten weeks, and afterwards half this amount. At his death, his family is entitled to eight pounds to defray the burial expences. This is a scale of liberality much greater than can be permanently maintained by such a rate of monthly contribution. As long as the generality of the members are young, the error is not discovered or felt, indeed so far from this being the case, benefit societies, for several years after their establishment, usually boast of greatly increasing funds.

At a later period, the expenditure is gradually augmented from an increase in the ratio of sickness and of deaths, in consequence of the advancing ages of the members: and the funds are then felt to be inadequate to the aggravated annual demand. To meet this, or adjust it to the existing ability of the society, many shifts are made, but seldom, if ever, with any permanent advantage. As soon as the difficulties of any friendly society are known, it ceases to be replenished by young and healthy members, who are the life and support of it, consequently the ultimate ruin of it is inevitable. Benefit societies are sometimes embarrassed by the roguery of an influential officer, running away with the greater part of the funds,—a circumstance which is not of very unfrequent occurrence. To prevent this and similar practices, the legislature, some years ago, passed an Act which affords ample protection to clubs disposed to take advantage of it. Few have, however enrolled themselves, owing to the same prejudice and suspicious feeling which have thrown difficulties in the path of our investigation.

The difference in the permanence of sick societies is occasioned by another circumstance of considerable influence, viz. *the greater or less respectability of the members.* Some clubs are composed exclusively of artisans, and others have a large proportion of master manufacturers, shopkeers, and persons of independent property. This is an important distinction. In the former, as soon as a member feels incapable of continuing his labours, he gives notice to his club, and draws weekly upon the funds. In the latter, many of the members, even when the illness is very protracted, never dream of falling back upon such resources. Again, in the one, imposition is frequently practised by needy and unprincipled members, and we are persuaded, occasionally to a great extent. Many flagrant instances have come under our own notice. In the other, such conduct is rare. The benefit societies, whose stock is large, generally belong to the latter description, and the members have pride in dilating on their large funds and a pleasure in promoting their increase.

Such is the high character of some clubs, that a person has to wait years before an opportunity occurs for his admission, the number being limited. The difficulty of entrance and the choice which such societies have of members, will clearly keep up a stream of the most respectable.

Enumeration of the Sick Clubs, or Friendly Societies, in the town and neighbourhood of Sheffield :—

Society.	Date when established.	No. of members.	Capital in 1840. £	Whether enrolled.
Old Union	1740	170	1040	not.
Young Society	1760	151	2967	not.
Tradesmen's	1761	931	4101	not.
Providence	1754	285	1990	not.
Green Foresters'	1761	...	...	...
Masons'.	1787	680	3060	Enrolled.
Revolution	1788	200	6708	not.
Prince of Wales'	1790	122	2461	Enrolled.
Scissorsmiths'	1791	250	2000	not.
Volunteers'	1794	250	...	not.
Female Benevolent	1805	470	2050	...
Jubilee	1809	300	5007	Enrolled.
Rockingham	1809	...	...	...
Silversmiths'	1811	256	1185	not.
Wesleyan	1813	199	2236	not.
Industrious	1814	74	625	not.
Waterloo	1815	...	...	not.
Norfolk	1819	200	...	not.
Olive branch	1819	...	...	...
Rock	1820	240	900	not.
Albion	1821	...	...	...
Fitzwilliam	1822	100	1222	Enrolled.
Resolution	1821	193	1345	not.
Bethell	1826	156	354	not.

P

Society.	Date when established.	No. of members.	Capital in 1840. £	Whether enrolled.
Surrey	1826	262	874	not.
Saint Patrick	1826	..	...	...
Marshall	1827	190	757	not.
Canning	1827	200	360	not.
Lord Brougham	1827	...	...	...
Mechanics'	1827	54	90	not.
Church of England	1828	234	1100	Enrolled.
Ebenezer	1828	102	387	not.
Rawson's	1828	55	559	...
Duke of Norfolk	1828	105	203	...
Wentworth	1829	...	...	...
T. A. Ward's	1829	80	200	...
Norfolk	1830	54	302	not
William IV.	1830	...	...	...
Birmingham Reform (late Tailors' Society)	1835	30	90	not.
Strickland	1835	65	220	not.
Charitable, or Gentlemens'	...	295	2274	not.
Prosperous or Young Shepherds	...	110	400	not.
Ecclesall New Friendly	...	430	3605	...
Independent	...	...	189	...
Braziers'	...	236	1440	not.
Radford	...	48	137	...
Filesmiths'	...	...	...	...
Crown	...	...	...	...
Beneficent	...	...	...	...
Rodney	...	...	...	...
Montgomery	...	49	375	...
Lord Milton	...	...	...	...
Fitzalan	...	83	334	...
Hanbey's Charity	...	...	...	...
Patriotic	...	70	150	...
Yorkshire Union	...	...	...	..

Classification of the ages of Members in nine of the following Sick Societies :—

Society.	Under 30.	30 to 39	40 to 49	50 to 59	60 to 69	70 and upwrds	Total.
Bethell	43	59	29	18	7	...	156
Church of England...	165	49	2	...	...	...	216
Fitzwilliam	26	42	30	2	...	...	100
Prince of Wales	40	20	19	28	12	3	122
Providence	81	80	76	25	22	4	288
Revolution	42	41	40	40	32	5	200
Scissorsmiths'..........	30	50	70	60	30	10	250
Tradesman's	101	269	241	182	98	18	909
Wesleyan	35	90	56	14	...	...	195
Totals	563	800	563	369	201	40	2436

Analysis of the Trades of the Members of the following Sick Societies :—

Trades, &c.	Prince of Wales.	Fitzwilliam.	Bethel.	Church of England.	Reform Birmingham.	Revolution.	Tradesmans'.	Total of each Trade.
Architects	...	...	...	...	...	1	...	1
Attorney	...	...	...	...	...	1	...	1
Auditor	...	...	...	...	...	1	...	1
Agent	...	...	...	...	...	1	...	1
Butchers	12	2	...	...	...	8	3	25
Button makers......	...	1	...	...	...	1	...	2
Bakers	...	...	...	...	...	7	...	7
Clerks	6	16	4	17	...	18	12	73
Coach makers	3	...	...	...	...	...	...	3
Casters	6	...	...	...	...	...	...	6
Comb makers	1	...	1	...	...	...	...	2
Carters	1	...	1	...	1	...	...	3
Cabinet case mkrs.	1	...	...	...	...	...	...	1
Chasers...............	...	...	...	...	...	3	...	3
Coopers..............	...	...	...	...	...	5	...	5
Carver and gilder...	...	...	...	...	...	1	...	1
Colliers	...	...	...	...	...	...	36	36
Coal leaders	...	...	...	...	...	...	5	5
Cutlers*	10	12	26	47	11	29	141	276

* Under the term cutlers, master manufacturers as well as journeymen are included; and the same may, also, be said of many of the other terms which designate the occupations of individuals.

F 2

Trades, &c.	Prince of Wales.	Fitzwilliam.	Bethel.	Church of England.	Reform Birmingham.	Revolution.	Trades men's.	Total of each Trade.
—— Fleam makers	1	...	...	...	...	...	...	1
—— Fork makers..	...	...	...	...	...	1	...	1
—— Haft pressers & horn cutters }	...	5	2	10	...	...	...	17
—— Razor makers	1	...	6	13	1	4	7	32
—— Scale cutters..	...	2	...	...	...	...	...	2
—— Scissorsmiths.	...	3	3	12	2	4	35	59
—— Shear makers	...	...	...	...	...	6	...	6
Die sinkers	...	3	...	...	...	2	...	5
Druggists	...	...	...	...	...	1	...	1
Edge-tool makers...	...	...	5	...	1	2	4	12
Engineers.............	2	...	...	...	...	...	...	2
File makers	2	...	6	19	2	3	43	75
Farmers	1	...	1	...	...	2	...	4
Fender makers......	1	2	6	...	...	3	3	15
Grocers	1	...	...	...	...	6	...	7
Glass cutters	1	...	...	...	...	...	...	1
Gentlemen	...	...	...	...	...	2	...	2
Grinders	...	...	22	6	...	...	79	107
Gardeners.............	...	...	...	...	...	...	2	2
Hair-dressers	...	...	1	...	...	...	...	1
Hatters.................	...	...	1	...	...	...	...	1
Ivory cutters.........	...	...	...	...	...	...	2	2
Ironmongers	1	...	...	...	...	...	...	1
Joiners	1	4	6	30	...	9	1	51
Joiners' tool makers	...	...	...	...	...	3	...	3
Labourers.............	...	...	15	...	...	1	39	55
Masons	2	...	7	8	...	...	2	19
Mercers	1	...	...	...	...	...	...	1
Moulders	1	...	2	...	...	...	...	3
Mark makers	1	2	...	...	...	...	...	3
Manufacturers	...	12	3	...	4	11	61	91
Maltsters	...	...	...	...	...	1	...	1
Opticians	2	...	...	...	...	...	...	2
Painters	...	2	1	...	...	2	...	5
Printers	...	12	...	...	...	3	...	15
Pawnbrokers	...	...	...	...	...	2	...	2
Plumbers & Glazrs.	...	...	...	...	...	2	2	4
Plasterers	...	...	...	...	...	1	...	1
Potters	...	...	...	...	...	2	...	2
Strickle makers ...	1	...	...	...	...	...	...	1
Saw makers	1	4	7	8	...	7	2	29

Trades, &c.	Prince of Wales.	Fitzwilliam.	Bethel.	Church of England.	Reform of Birmingham.	Revolution.	Trades-men's.	Total of each Trade.
Shopkeepers.........	...	4	...	...	1	...	11	16
Snuffer makers......	...	...	1	...	...	...	...	1
Stationers............	...	...	...	...	...	1	...	1
Saddlers	...	...	...	...	...	4	...	4
Sculptors	...	...	...	...	...	1	...	1
Schoolmasters	...	...	...	...	...	2	...	2
Steel refiners	...	...	...	...	...	3	10	13
Surgeons	...	...	...	...	...	2	...	2
Silversmiths.........	11	6	...	22	3	8	12	62
Shoemakers	12	1	5	...	...	3	8	29
Tailors	3	3	1	...	...	1	7	15
Type founders	1	1	1	...	...	1	2	6
Tilters & forgemen..	...	...	9	...	...	...	30	39
White metalsmiths.	16	...	8	8	3	...	...	35
Wood turners	3	...	2	...	...	2	...	7
White & blacksmiths	1	...	2	12	...	2	...	17
Wheelwrights	1	...	...	...	...	1	...	2
Watchmaker	...	...	...	...	...	1	...	1
Victuallers	6	1	1	...	1	4	...	13

It was our intention, when this inquiry was first suggested, to present the same valuable facts with respect to the rest of the clubs, but the untoward and illiberal opposition experienced prevented this being accomplished. The facts would have been important on various considerations. It would then have been easy to ascertain the relation between different rates of wages and the disposition to provide against the necessities of the future, and, also, the relation between different degrees of intelligence manifested by different classes of artisans, and such a disposition of forethought. The habits of these classes are very dissimilar, owing to the nature of their employments, the remuneration which they yield, and many other circumstances; and if the information sought had been obtained, there would have been abundant data for more elaborate inquiries, which would have afforded, in conjunction with the previous researches, just and comprehensive views on the numerous causes influencing the condition of the working classes.

Names and number of Members of Secret Orders of Sheffield and its Vicinity :—

Odd Fellows' Lodges connected with the Manchester Unity.	Full Benefit Members.*	Odd Fellows' Lodges connected with the Manchester Unity.	Full Benefit Members.*
Amicable	63	Poor Man's Guardian...	77
Ancient Abbey	92	Promoter of Peace	65
Archangel	72	Queen Victoria	32
Benevolent	97	Rockingham	40
Botanic	51	Royal Oak	57
Britain's Reformation...	24	Saint Mary's	49
Britannia	70	Social Design	65
Earl Fitzwilliam.........	64	Star of Providence	84
Favourite..................	209	Travellers' Home	22
Foresters' (two Lodges)	60	Travellers' Rest	25
Foundation stone	181	Waterloo...................	60
Good Intent	65		
Good Samaritan..........	128	OTHER SECRET ORDERS	
Lily of the valley	175		
Lord Nelson	59	The Druids...............	—
Mechanics'	41	The Freemasons..........	—
Miners' Refuge	44	The Philanthropic } Brotherhood......... }	130
Morning Star	92		
Norfolk	54	The Rhecabites	40
Philanthropic	323	The Tesserians	70

* In addition to these numbers, about one-fifth more are members but not entitled to full benefit.

Imperfect as these tables are, we are not aware that the same particulars have been furnished by any other town, consequently it is not in our power to institute any comparison between the provident habits of artisans in this district and those of any other, as shown by the proportion in sick clubs and other societies. From partial returns which have been made it would appear, that the proportion here is far greater than is exhibited by any other manufacturing town in relation to the existing population.

The number of clubs is 56. The members in 39 only, amount to 7,978, and the stock belonging to 38 clubs is £53,373. There are 17 societies, of which we were not able to procure any particulars, and 18, of whose funds no account is rendered. It is probable that the total number of members is about 11,000, and the accumulated stock at least £70,000. The funds of one club,* which are not stated, are known to exceed those of any of the enumerated societies. The number of secret orders is 36, the number of members in 34, is 2,980.

These facts are pleasing to contemplate. They show, on the part of the labouring classes generally, a forethought and consideration which do them infinite credit, and we hope that the increasing opportunities for acquiring knowledge, will be accompanied with greater sobriety and the manifestation of a higher tone of morality. The investigation of their condition, and the study of various circumstances in which they are placed, have left upon the mind many grateful impressions, and though there is much to regret and condemn in their conduct, there is nevertheless a large amount of shrewd common sense, sterling independence and unswerving honesty to admire. The working classes, as a body, in this town, with the exception of the grinders, are superior in intelligence and physical condition to those of any other manufacturing district. This superiority, for which we contend, is to be traced to the great diversity of the occupations, and the comparatively slight degree to which machinery interferes with manual labour. The extensive introduction of it is not favourable to the exercise and development of the mental faculties. Wherever it is largely employed, the artisan is not only saved the necessity of speculative and active thought, without which the understanding stagnates, but he becomes the slave of its motions, inured to long hours, and cheapened in his value by its untiring competitive exertions.

* The Rodney.

Table exhibiting the duration of Sickness or Incapacity, in days per annum, at different nominal ages, in the Silversmiths' Benefit Society and the Fitzwilliam Society, compared with similar results deduced from the published Returns of the Scottish Benefit Societies, Mr. Finlaison's collections and Mr. Ansell's Tables.

AGE.	Silversmiths.	Fitzwilliam.	Scottish Societies.	Mr. Finlaison's	Mr. Ansell's.
20	5.41	1.18	3.32	6.11	5.46
25	5.51	1.22	3.85	6.34	5.72
30	5.69	1.28	4.65	6.74	6.15
35	6.04	1.43	5.72	7.42	6.85
40	6.71	1.73	7.22	8.60	8.02
45	7.98	2.37	9.29	10.64	9.97
50	10.40	3.72	12.17	14.16	13.19
55	15.02	6.59	16.17	20.23	18.52
60	23.81	12.66	21.72	30.74	27.37
65	40.55	25.47	29.44	48.89	42.02
70	72.45	52.70	40.16	80.23	66.32
75	133.17	110.75	55.05	134.38	106.72
80	248.95	231 53	75.48	227.92	173.55

We obtained with considerable difficulty the facts, on which the duration of sickness is calculated, in the two clubs specified. The Fitzwilliam society affords no average data. It was established so late as 1822, and has only 101 members, the rule of the club being not to increase more than two members annually. The gain for the past ten years, on each member per month, has been 1s. 2¼d., while the monthly contribution has been only 1s. 6d. The members are either young or in the prime of life, and are among the most respectable of the artisans, consequently are less likely to simulate sickness, or on any trifling occasion to make a demand on the funds. The silversmiths' society was established in 1811, has a greater number of members, and many of these are much more aged than in the Fitzwilliam society, hence the calculations may be regarded as founded upon fair average data, and do not differ, in any important degree, from those in the two last columns.

The changes in the number of members, and the amount paid in time of sickness in eight years, in the following Sick or Benefit Societies.

NAME OF CLUB.	NUMBER OF MEMBERS							
	1835	1836	1837	1838	1839	1840	1841	1842
Prince of Wales'	120	120	120	120	120	120	115	114
The Charitable	319	302	304	297	295	286	270	252
The Norfolk+	200	200	200	200	200	200	200	200
The Tradesmen's	1150	1120	1080	1070	1007	930	840	750
Lord Brougham	205	213	220	226	211	205	203	160
The Silversmiths'	279	273	271	263	263	256	260	266
The Masons'	732	725	710	693	687	650	640	610
Olive Branch	179	191	194	198	197	193	189	184

AMOUNT PAID.

	Prince of Wales.			The Chritabl.			The Norfolk.			The Tradsmns.			Lord Broughm			The Silvr-smiths'.			The Masons.			Olive Branch.		
	£	s.	d.	£	s.	d.	£	s.	d.	£	s.	d.	£	s.	d.	£	s.	d.	£	s.	d.	£	s.	d.
1835	139	3	0	300	0	0	117	8	10	840	10	0	105	16	5	222	12	0	750	0	0	90	0	0
1836	163	11	0	308	6	0	118	8	8	820	6	0	79	18	7	297	3	0	798	5	0	125	0	0
1837	170	16	0	290	5	0	160	12	10	1024	3	6	138	1	1	205	5	0	762	10	0	110	0	0
1838	138	18	0	327	1	6	157	7	2	955	16	6	127	16	11	195	2	6	738	0	0	109	0	0
1839	242	8	0	354	7	6	169	15	5	1034	15	6	79	7	11	151	5	10	630	11	0	122	0	0
1840	202	6	9	436	4	6	153	2	4	1132	10	6	143	11	0	146	9	3	738	9	0	107	15	0
1841	222	18	0	451	5	6	169	9	4	826	16	+0	148	4	9	132	1	8	781	10	0	121	5	0
1842	164	18	9‡	356	10	7	172	6	4	835	17	0	140	17	9	167	2	6	713	16	0	140	6	0

We procured the foregoing particulars in order to ascertain the influence of prosperous and adverse times on the condition of sick clubs, and they are worthy of consideration. We observe, with one exception, where the number of members is not fixed, that for the past five or six years, the numerical strength of these societies has gradually declined, and in some cases to a great extent, while the amount paid to sick members has very greatly increased, with the exception of one class—the silversmiths. The decrease in the numbers is indisputable evidence of the serious reduction in the ability of the artisan to maintain his independence—the increase in the sums paid, of

* This club is limited to 200 members, and has always candidates on the books for admission.

+ In 1841 and 1842 the allowance to sick members was reduced 1s. per week, making in the year a difference of about £120.

‡ These sums are for sickness and mortality.

the progress of disease from the same circumstance. In the tradesmen's society, which from the number and character of its members, being almost entirely artisans, affords the best evidence of the influence of the times, we perceive that in eight years the members have decreased from 1150 to 750 ; and in 1840, previously to diminishing the payments to sick members, the payments had increased from £840. 10s. to £1132. 10s. 6d. The other clubs exhibit similar results. Such changes shew the serious interruptions which are constantly taking place to the steady progress of social improvements. The inability to remain in a sick club, is not only evidence of a diminution in the power of commanding the necessaries of life, but of a corresponding degradation in the moral tone of the mind, and out of this spring ignorance, recklessness and crime.

CHAPTER XVIII.

THE AMOUNT OF RELIGIOUS INSTRUCTION AND EDUCATION IN THE SEVERAL TOWNSHIPS OF THE SHEFFIELD UNION.

The subject to which we first direct attention, is the consideration of the existing means of education for a rapidly increasing population. No portion of our labours is, perhaps, equal to this in importance, and yet until lately it has received comparatively little attention. While immense progress has been made in the extension of manufactures, as well as in the accumulation of wealth in numerous hands, there has been no proportionately increased anxiety to diminish the abounding ignorance, by presenting greater facilities of education for the rising generation. It is true that religious bodies without distinction, have shown a praiseworthy solicitude in the establishment of Sunday Schools; and we are ready to admit that they have been instruments of great good, at the same time they are altogether inadequate to the urgent demands of the times. The knowledge imparted by them is exceedingly superficial; and the few hours which children remain under instruction or superintendence per week, scarcely allow of the reception of impressions calculated to modify the character. For the little good which they effect we are grateful, and they richly deserve encouragement. We proceed now to state the number and variety of the schools, and, also, the number of pupils in each. The information was accurately given to 1838,* and subsequent inquiries in 1840-1, exhibited no material alterations in the facts.

SUNDAY SCHOOLS.	SCHOOLS.	SCHOLARS.
Established Church	25	2758
Wesleyan	26	3914
New Connexion	8	1450
Calvinist	14	2208
Primitive Methodists	2	140
Wesleyan Association	4	263
Baptists	2	290
Unitarians	2	189
		11,212
PUBLIC DAY SCHOOLS.		
Established Church	8	466
National	18	2437
Infant	8	522
Schools not classed	...	245
Wesleyan	12	1051
Lancasterian	2	1140
Ditto Infant	1	175
Calvinist	1	52
Baptist, Infant	1	100
		6,188
PRIVATE OR GENERAL DAY SCHOOLS.		
Superior	81	1273
Middling (Day and Evening) ...	22	1019
Common (Ditto)	27	1130
Dame Schools	46	1037
	177	4,459
		21,859

* In this year, the Rev. Dr. Sutton, Vicar, investigated the subject.

SUMMARY.	MALES	FEMALES.
Under 5 years of age............	633	561
5 to 14	10,622	9135
15 and upwards	384	179
	11,639	9,875
		21,514
Two Infant Schools not classed		345
Total		21,859

Number of Children on the books of the Public Day and Sabbath Schools, in the entire parish of Sheffield, in December, 1840 :—

SUNDAY SCHOOLS.	SCHOOLS.	SCHOLARS.
Church of England	38	3901
Wesleyan Methodist	25	4034
Roman Catholic	2	181
Independent and Calvinist.........	18	2394
Unitarian	2	226
New Connexion Methodist.........	5	1093
Methodist Association	4	280
Primitive Methodists	2	169
Baptist	4	626
	100	12,904

PUBLIC DAY SCHOOLS.		
Endowed	8	407
Church of England..................	24	3345
Wesleyan Methodist	5	700
Lancasterian	2	1114
Roman Catholic	2	133
	41	5699

Summary of the Pupils in Public Day Schools,	5699
in Private Schools	4459
in Infant Schools	797
Total	10,955

The following table presents several interesting facts bearing on this subject :—*

Names of the day-schools visited.	Average daily attendance.	No. on books.	Average duration stay in School. Yrs. Mo.		No. present when visited	Of these could read fairly.	Of these could write fairly.
National S., Carver st., Boys	370	430	*1	9	246	140	100
Ditto, ditto. Girls..........	350	380	1	9	170	100	80
St. Mary's Church, Boys' S.	160	219	1	6	146	80	60
Ditto, ditto, Girls' School ..	190	294	1	7	170	110	95
St. Georges' Church Boys' S	135	203	1	2	164	78	58
Ditto, ditto, Girls..........	9.	130	0	8	77	34	30
St John's Church, Boys' S.	160	230	1	3	150	70	60
+Lancasterian Boys School..	385	554	1	0	360	200	141
Ditto Girls' School	400	560	1	3	300	200	100
Brunswick Meth, Boys' S..	150	200	1	0	145	61	36
Ditto, ditto, Girls' School ..	90	155	0	6	104	80	23
Red hill Methodist, Boys ..	74	150	0	8	63	22	20
Roman Catholic, Boys	60	68	0	6	42	17	15
Ditto, ditto, Girls	45	65	0	6	23	8	3
Church Infant School, Boys and Girls	200	250	‡0	0	107	28	9
	2859	3888	15	1	2267	1228	829

* Exclusive of 30 children in the alphabet class.

+ These schools admit all denominations.

‡ Not stated.

From this table it appears, that 26.47 per cent. of the whole are continually absent, and that the average stay at school is 13 months: but this summarily discounted for continual absence leaves only 9½ months as the average total attendance.†

The effective amount of education may also be considered under a different view. The centesimal value of non-attendance may be applied to the pupilage numerically,

* See the report of J. C. Symons, Esq., on the moral and physical condition of the children employed in the trades of Sheffield.

† In the column headed "Average duration of stay at School," the result should have been stated as an average of the fourteen given terms, which is one year one month. If the " duration" means the interval between the entrance to and the final departure from school, this will be modified by the continual absence, which is 26.47 per cent., making the total attendance of each individual on an average 9½ months only.

to ascertain the value of constant attendance, independently of stay at school. Discounting at the above rate, we find that of the 10,955 only 8055 may be considered as constantly attending for the 13 months. We have not, however, the census of the population of Sheffield, distinguishing the ages. In this dilemma we resort to the nearly parallel case of Manchester, from the distributive census of which we infer, that the number of children between the ages of three and fourteen, are about 22½ per cent. of the total population. Hence the number of boys and girls who ought to be in a state of pupilage, will be found to be about 24,750, so that not one-third of the youth of Sheffield can be regarded as receiving any education at all.

From. very different data of the population and the distribution of it with respect to age, it is not a little singular that Mr. Symons arrives at the same conclusion :—

" The population of Sheffield," he remarks, " is now 97,000 ; of these it is believed that one-fourth are under 14 years of age. There will therefore be 24,250 children. According to the number of births compared with the infant deaths, there are about 6,000 children under three years old. Of the remaining 18,250 children, at least two-thirds belong to the working-classes. Above 12,000 children, therefore, of the working classes are of an age at which they ought to be receiving education at day-schools. *Scarcely one-third of this number*, as appears from the above facts, are even able to read fairly, and *not one-half attend day schools at all.* This estimate is so thoroughly corroborated by the most trustworthy evidence I have received, that I entertain the belief that *two-thirds of the working class children are growing up in a state of comparative ignorance."*

The foregoing facts present no very favourable picture of the condition of the rising generation; nor when studied will it be a matter of surprise that crime, dissipation and immorality of every kind should increase with the extension of manufactures and the creation of wealth. To the man who is in the enjoyment of the luxuries of life, and whose associations suggest ease and independence, how natural it is to expatiate in glowing terms on the vast progress of civilization! He looks little beyond himself and his class. The narrowness of his vision and the selfishness of his heart, exclude from contemplation the struggling wretchedness and the gross ignorance of the masses. If his command of all that ministers to the senses were the measure of such progress, we might permit him the indulgence of his imagination. If by the progress of civilization is implied, however, the happiness of the people, the determination of this measure will require the analysis of many circumstances. His own is only one element in the calculation.

We trust the facts to which we have directed attention will awaken the few to a sense of the duties which they owe to the many. It is good to build Churches, but a preparatory step is necessary—to impart the principles of knowledge, and these will not shoot up in the understanding simply from the increased facilities of worship. We must first teach the mind to think—supply it with the means of thought, and thus a basis of intelligence will be formed for the reception of religious impressions. The union of the two will confer a much larger amount of benefit upon society than either alone. The impressions without intellectual light, is the mind groping in darkness after good, in which many of the highest faculties are

untouched—many of the finest susceptibilities of our nature
unawakened. The universe in all its magnificence of
design—its teeming relations to man, is felt only by the
educated understanding. To excite admiration of the
works of creation, is to arouse a spirit which is instinct
with adoration, and which breathes the ennobling principles
of liberality and christian charity.

*Number of Churches and Chapels of the Established
Church, with the extent of their accommodation :—*

Place.	Name of Church.	No. of Churches.	Capable of containing.	No. of Chapels.	Capable of containing.
Sheffield Township.	St. Peter's	1	1500	—	—
————	St. Paul's......	1	1400	—	—
————	St. James's....	1	800	—	—
————	St. George's...	1	2000	—	—
————	St. Mary's	1	2000	—	—
————	St Philip's....	1	2000	—	—
————	St. John's	1	1170	—	—
————	Hospital chapl	—	—	1	300
Chaplry of Attercliffe.	Christ church.	1	2000	1	0*
Ecclesall	————	—	—	1	700
Crookes	————	1	600	—	—
Fullwood	————	1	540	—	—
Darnall	————	—	—	1	400
	Total accommodation...		14010		1400

* Used only for funeral service.

Number and denomination of Dissenting Places of Worship, with the extent of their accommodation.

DENOMINATION.	Township of Sheffield.		CHAPELRY of ATTERCLIFFE				Parish of Handsworth.	
			Township of Attercliffe-cum-Darnall.		Township of Brightside Bierlow.			
	No	Sittings.	No	Sittings.	No	Sittings.	No	Sittings.
Wesleyan Methdst.	4	5600	2	750	2	1420	1	350
Meth. N. Connexn.	1	900	1	350				
Meth. Association..	1	500						
Independent Meth.					1	200		
Independent	6	4980	2	800			2	600
Baptist...............	2	1050						
Unitarian.............	1	915						
Roman Catholic ...	1	800						
Quakers	1	1000					1	130
Israelites	1	350						
Totals	18	16095	5	1900	3	1620	4	1080
Estimated Population, 1838 ...	67,628		15,500				2700	

Great exertions have been made and successfully within the past few years to increase the means of religious instruction, especially by the Church, the Methodists and the Independents, and such are now amply provided in the most populous and needy districts. Many of the places of worship are very indifferently attended, indeed in many cases the accommodation has been multiplied greatly beyond the demand of the several sects. A spirit of rivalry has animated many of these to erect much larger and more expensive edifices than were required, and far beyond their ability to pay for the cost incurred; hence several are in difficulties, or very much embarrassed in consequence of their zeal having overstepped their judgment. If the same enterprise had shown itself in the endeavour first to educate the rising generation—to dissipate the ignorance which pervades the masses, the religious accommodation would have been necessary. The zeal, has unquestionably done good, but it began where it ought to have terminated. The world is much less in need of proselytism than intelligence. Indeed the progress of the former should flow, as a natural result, from the advancement of the latter, otherwise bigotry, intolerance and all uncharitableness are liable to be associated, to the neglect of virtues in which society is much more concerned than in individual belief.

The artisans generally are not frequent attendants on a place of worship. It is stated, on authority which is the result of inquiry, that not one family in twenty is in the practice of visiting either Church or Chapel, indeed it is a duty in the performance of which the working classes are exceedingly lax, and the evil is not to be cured by the creation of religious accommodation.

There is one circumstance in the table which requires explanation, viz. the apparently very limited accommodation for the Catholic portion of the population. It may, however, be regarded as double what the figures indicate. It is usual to repeat the religious service twice on the Sunday, in order to meet the wants of a numerous congregation, so that accommodation is created for twice the number of individuals stated in the returns. The Catholics here, bear a much less proportion to the whole population than in most other manufacturing towns. The immigration of the Irish to this district is comparatively small, the various branches of trade carried on not admitting of their employment in the same degree as the manufactures in other places.

Q 2.

In 1767 the Catholics in this town were 319,* at this time they are about 5,500; 2,200 signed the petition against the recently proposed Bill of Ministers, for the better education of the young in manufacturing districts; and so greatly have they augmented of late, that it is in contemplation to erect an additional place of worship on an extensive scale. This demand does not arise entirely from immigration, or from the natural increase of the resident families, but from the extension of Catholicism. The Clergy have been men of unwearied exertion, courteous in bearing and of unblemished character, and their duties have been performed with a degree of faithfulness, that has won esteem and regard even from bitter opponents. We speak from a personal knowledge of them. And we cannot help placing on record our regret, that a difference of opinion on religion should be accompanied with persecution in multifarious forms, a disgrace to the age and a satire on the imagined progress of civilization. The conviction of right in regard to belief, should inspire an instinctive tendency towards the contemplation of the Deity, and from the study of his attributes a spirit of charity and benevolence should be evolved, as unconfined as the light which pervades the universe.

As an impartial historian of the existing state of things, we are called upon to allude to one religious denomination, that might be deemed best to pass over with contempt, we allude to the Israelites—the followers of Johanna Southcote, all of whose predictions were false and herself an imposter. Had experience not taught us that no doctrines are too gross or absurd for mankind to entertain,

* This included the Catholics in the town and neighbourhood.

the continued existence of such a sect would be inexplicable. Man is, however, a believing animal and not by nature sceptical, and will hold to something with extraordinary tenacity, and the firmer the more he is opposed. In the expression of our sentiments let us not do injustice to the followers of a doctrine which we have no wish to dwell upon. In their dress they are neat, in conduct sober and exemplary, in their attendance on religious worship regular, and their families present an appearance of comfort and independence, in striking contrast with the condition of the artisans generally.

CHAPTER XIX.

THE CHURCH OF ENGLAND INSTRUCTION SOCIETY.

This society was established in 1839, somewhat on the principles of the mechanics' institute, with this difference, however, that religious instruction is blended with the various departments of knowledge taught. Classes are formed for the purpose of teaching the following subjects :

1. Writing and mental arithmetic.
2. Arithmetic.
3. Geography and history.
4. Reading.
5. Theology.
6. Catechetical theology.
7. English grammar.
8. Drawing.
9. Mechanics in general.

Monthly public lectures are usually given, and mostly by the Clergy of the town and neighbourhood. Singing and prayer precede each lecture. The number of members is about 220, and we regret that they are principally honorary. The lectures are in general on natural history, natural philosophy, ecclesiastical polity, sacred biography, biblical knowledge and other kindred subjects. The object contemplated in the formation of the society, was to afford general knowledge to the artisan, and at the same time to produce religious impressions, a prejudice being entertained against the Mechanics' Institute, from the latter being altogether excluded from the scheme of instruction. It must be admitted that the combination of the two is always desirable when practicable, but in many cases it would be attended with insuperable difficulties, and certainly could not be carried out in the Mechanics' Institute, the members being of different religious sentiments. In justice to the clergy we must state, that they have been indefatigible in their exertions to render the society useful, and among them are men of considerable scientific and literary attainments. They are, without exception, exemplary in their conduct and zealous in the performance of their duties.

In addition to the public lectures and classes, a philosophical section has recently been formed which holds its meetings monthly, on which occasion papers are read on geology, botany, mineralogy, political economy, moral philosophy, history, the arts, or on ecclesiastical history. These meetings are open to all the members, except to those of the various classes, who are not regarded as sufficiently advanced to feel an interest in the investigation of subjects elaborately treated. The society has, also, the attraction of a museum, which though not particularly rich in numerous objects of natural history or of antiquities, has many that are rare and of considerable interest. This society from the manner in which it is conducted deserves the support of all, who are anxious to improve the condition of the rising generation; and it is greatly to be regretted, that both this and the Mechanics' institute are crippled in their endeavours to do good from want of more liberal encouragement.

CHAPTER XX.

MECHANICS' INSTITUTION.

In the previous inquiries we have clearly shown the deficiency of education among the working classes, the fact is indeed painful from its magnitude and the numerous evils of which it is the source. Various exertions have been made to provide instruction, and especially to interest the feelings of the artisan in schemes having for their object his improvement. Mechanics' Institutions were regarded, at the time of their formation, as well calculated to awaken his attention, professing to teach what is useful in connexion with the arts and sciences, and the government of such institutions being mainly in the hands of his own class. That they have effected good is undeniable, but it is, also, equally true, that the amount is much less than was anticipated. Those for whom they were designed have not been roused to participate largely in the proffered advantages. The institution established in this town began under favourable auspices. It had the support of the wealthy and intelligent, not only in a pecuniary point of view, but the zealous co-operation of some as public lecturers and teachers; but if the number of members be any criterion of success, the following facts will show that the institution has retrograded rather than advanced. It was established in 1833 :—

Year.	Honorary Members.	Members.	Apprentices.	Total.
1833	100	320	280	700
1834	120	250	160	530
1835	110	210	180	500
1836	120	200	210	533
1837	127	210	150	487
1838	114	194	125	433
1839	116	206	168	490
1840	110	158	220	488
1841	108	166	172	446
1842*	114	184	235	533

The following subjects were taught the first year :—Reading, arithmetic, geography, grammar, drawing, mathematics, and algebra; philosophy of the human mind, Latin and French.

A series of questions was addressed to an individual, who from his intelligence and practical knowledge of the institution, was well qualified to furnish the required information, and the subjoined answers were kindly given—

1. What number of pupils, in the first and each successive year, could neither read nor write?

About one in two hundred could not read, and forty were incapable of writing.

2. What proportion of those attending each year, of the higher classes of instruction, had received a respectable education?

About one-half.

* In this year a Library was established in connexion with the Institution, which explains the increase of members.

3. What number of public lectures has been given annually from the commencement?

Average thirty-five.

4. What number of persons attend each public lecture?

About two hundred males and one hundred females.

5. Are the expenses of the public lectures defrayed by the members, or can any person, on the payment of sixpence, have the privilege of attending?

About three-fourths of the expenses are defrayed by the members.

6. Have any of the pupils distinguished themselves by their proficiency?

Some, whose acquirements were very limited on entering the institution, made such progress as to become teachers of grammar, geography and drawing.

7. What is the number of paid and gratuitous teachers, at this time?

The paid teachers, four; the gratuitous, six.

8. What are the fees paid by members and pupils, and what are the privileges which they enjoy?

Boys or apprentices pay 3s. half-yearly, in advance, and entrance 1s. 6d. A higher class of members pay 4s. half-yearly, and 2s. 6d. entrance. A third class pay 10s. 6d. annually, without any entrance. The privileges for these subscriptions, are attendance on the public lectures, admission to the reading, writing, arithmetic, geography, grammar, mathematical, algebraic, and latin classes. Extra fees are paid for attendance on the drawing, natural philosophy, and French classes.

9. What reason is to be assigned for the decline of the institution, from the period of its establishment?

The causes, in my opinion are three:—1. The institution has to depend too much on gratuitous teachers, whose exertions are not always continuous or regular, and hence not efficient. 2. The instruction furnished is too scientific, abstract and serious. The feelings of the uneducated are not interested, because the understanding does not comprehend what is taught. 3. The frequent vicissitudes of prosperity and depression to which the working classes are subject. Prosperity begets dissipation, idleness and a vicious indulgence of the appetite. Depression, the diminution of wages,—misery,—a disregard of self, and often the necessity of increased bodily exertion for an inadequate remuneration.

On the formation of this institution we had the honour to be President, and held the office several years, and for a considerable period took a warm and active interest in its welfare. We regret that it has not been encouraged by the class for which it was designed. For the failure we should assign another reason in addition to the foregoing, viz., the want of more education in the young and artisans generally to appreciate the advantages of such an institution. The teaching and lectures appeal to minds that have made some progress in knowledge, and will not, after the novelty is worn off, create a permanent interest. The remark of our friend with respect to gratuitous teaching is perfectly correct. It is seldom efficient, and yet, unfortunately, the funds are too limited to pay individuals well qualified for the important duties of instruction. All such institutions should be supported by Government, and have assistance in the form of annual grants. A few hundred pounds given to each town, for the payment of teachers and lecturers, would be productive of inestimable benefits.

CHAPTER XXI.

MECHANICS' LIBRARY.

The Mechanics' Library has no connexion whatever with the Mechanics' Institution. Attempts have been made to unite the two, but without success. It must not be inferred from the title that it is entirely supported by mechanics or persons in humble circumstances. The excellence of the works which it contains and the easy terms on which the use of them can be enjoyed, induce many highly respectable families to become subscribers. An examination of the following table will show how large a proportion of the subscribers are in *good* circumstances, by which is implied various degrees above the condition of artisans. It was orginally established for the benefit of this class, and we regret that they are not the chief supporters of it. We do not object to others participating in the advantages, but we prefer these being enjoyed by the artisan whose means and opportunities for acquiring information are exceedingly limited.

YEAR.	Honorary Subscribers.	Apprentices.	Subscribers in good circumstances.	Annual subscriptions of Apprentices.	Number of Volumes.	Average increase.
				s.		
Dec. 27th 1823*						
1824	68	22	234	4	913	—
1825	71	37	308	4	1100	187
{ 1826	50	60	400	4	1580 }	600
{ do. July	—	111	411	4	1700 }	
1827	45	123	347	4	2038	338
1828	40	110	304	4	2246	208
1829	40	149	374	4	2481	235
1830	31	165	359	4	2752	271
1831	38	186	375	4	3018	266
1832	40	103	384	4	3246	228
1833	45	185	411	4	3543	297
1834	41	149	447	4	3747	204
1835	41	205	505	4	3937	190
1836	44		627	4	4215	278
1837	46		659	4	4554	339
1838	41		633	4	4750	196
1839	46		743	4	4900	150
1840	55		620	4	5167	267
1841	55		636	4	5328	161
1842	55		643	4	5628	300

The annual income of the library is about £220, and at least half of this sum is expended yearly in the purchase of books, so that at no distant period it will contain a greater variety of works than any similar establishment in the town. It is managed with economy and sound judgment, and every care has been taken to secure works of admitted excellence.

The amount of good which the library is annually conferring is unquestionably great. The labouring classes for whom the institution was especially designed, are not, however, found to be chief participators in the benefits

* This is the time when the public meeting was held, at which the Library was instituted : it was not opened until 1824, April 12.

of it. Novels are interdicted, and in our opinion with propriety. Several determined struggles have been made to introduce them, but in vain. The plea has been, that many productions of this character are admirable for the knowledge of human nature which they convey, and unobjectionable in point of morality. This of course is admitted, but where there is one novel that ought to be on the shelves of the Mechanics' Library, there are fifty that would be out of place there, and which after a few years would not be worth the space they occupy. We are not advocates for placing in the hands of the young, whether artisans or youth in a higher position in society, works of fiction too frequently bordering on questionable morality. We are not insensible of the necessity of interesting the feelings in early life, and even to a certain extent by productions in which imagination plays an important part, but the imagination in this case should be the medium by which sound information or valuable facts are communicated. The opinion which is expressed with respect to novels and works of this class, is in reference solely to the Mechanics' Library, the subscribers to which are supposed to have little time at command, and therefore this little should be applied towards the acquisition of sound information. Any member is at liberty to propose a book, but the admission or rejection of it rests with the committee, which is elected annually at a public meeting, and likewise all officers connected with the institution.

CHAPTER XXII.

THE LITERARY AND PHILOSOPHICAL SOCIETY.

———

In the year 1822, the combined efforts of a few distinguished individuals led to the establishment of this institution, and fortunately for its welfare many have been spared to render it their steady and valuable support to the present time. When the extent of the population of the town and neighbourhood is considered,—the variety of the manufactures carried on,—and the importance of a knowledge of the arts to the successful prosecution of them, as well as the wealth and enterprise with which they are associated, it would be imagined that a society of this kind would meet with very warm encouragement. Painful, however, it is to confess, that the manufacturers and the merchants generally, show little solicitude either for their own improvement or that of their families, if such solicitude is to be measured by the countenance given to an institution, the object and tendency of which is to create an interest in philosophical and literary pursuits. If the consideration of their own advantage furnished no motive to aid its exertions, the reflection that its labours are calculated, in an eminent degree, to benefit the town, should supply a sufficient inducement.

We have in various parts of this inquiry stated, that the extension of manufactures is much less favourable to the cultivation of literary and scientific pursuits than would be imagined from the wealth which results. This when rapidly created, is almost invariably associated with a disposition to external display, which manifests itself in every possible form, and is supposed to be necessary to maintain a certain position in society. The universal struggling after the means which give this position, and the prevailing conviction that wealth alone gives it, concentrate the purposes and feelings of the mind in one direction only, to the exclusion of the cultivation of the taste and the relaxation of overwrought energies, a fitting repose for which would be found in the contemplation of natural objects, or in literary and scientific inquiries. The tendencies of the age, however, admit of no repose. Perhaps, there never was a period in the history of this country when intellectual excellence, except it ministered to the vitiated appetites of the times, or showed itself in connexion with increased facilities for the creation of wealth, was either less appreciated or less liberally rewarded. Men who have devoted their days and nights towards the extension of the boundaries of knowledge, who have laboured to improve both the head and the heart of the rising generation, secure no position commensurate with their talents. They are too frequently viewed as visionaries—men who have no just idea of the practical duties of life, by which is understood not the cultivation of the understanding, but the determined application of the whole man in the chase after riches. Religion itself becomes a subordinate object, except as a means of worldly aggrandisement or a matter of policy.

Fashion and interest unfortunately mix themselves up with sacred as well as profane things, and indeed to such a melancholy extent, that talents, acquirements and virtues are measured not according to their just value, but according to the religious opinions with which they may be associated.

Persecution certainly does not show itself as in former times bearing the axe or the fire-brand, but what it has lost in the concentration and harshness of its spirit, it has gained in the refinement and multiplication of its manifestations. It pervades the whole contexture of society, dividing the religious community not simply into parties, but making the line of demarcation broad and ragged. It permits no blending of the one into the other, as in the shades of a well executed picture, not even in the social intercourse of society. Each sect has its standard of truth, and every departure from it, whether in the direction of believing more or less than this standard, is treated not with silent indifference, or indeed in the largeness of that spirit which Christianity inculcates, but with a narrow and illiberal feeling petty in the extreme in its displays. It shows itself not only in the thousand preferences which it suggests, founded on party distinctions, but in a bitter and undefined sentiment of hostility that in a variety of forms, touches with unerring accuracy its object.

The expression of such a spirit is not favourable to the independent exercise of thought—to that freedom of action essential to the progress of mind and the advancement of the race. It holds out a premium to dissimulation and hypocrisy, by chalking out the direction in which success may be attained, not by talents or virtues, but by the

R

assumption of opinions in which there is no merit, except as being the result of rigid investigation.

The evil is injurious by giving a tendency to the mind to attach importance to subtile distinctions, instead of mental qualities or virtues which ought to exercise a pre-eminent influence, and which should be judged, not by a standard of religious opinion, which is adjusted by prejudice, but with one in harmony with the nature of the objects themselves. So inconsistent is this spirit, that it almost becomes bland and courteous towards those who believe nothing, compared with its bitterness against individuals, whose whole life has been a series of noble and disinterested exertions to benefit mankind, exhibiting in their conduct, active virtues and high-toned principles of morality in association with religion.

The perversion of the judgment and the unreasonableness of its requirements, is not less absurd than the antiquated taste, of which we may see some traces at the present day, which fashioned trees into grotesque figures. Cramp not the energies of nature, nor restrain the freedom of its manifestations except when wayward or fraught with evils. Allow it to have ample space for the exercise of its diversified powers, as long as it respects the great principles of morality. The exquisite beauty of human nature—the variety of its faculties and impulses, like that of the noble tree, is marred according as either is forced to assume temporary and uncongenial forms—forms against which nature instinctively struggles to be free, and when she fails, man becomes not what he seems, and the tree stunted in its growth and abridged of its fair proportions stands a melancholy spectacle of bad taste.

This splitting up of the religious community into numerous sects, united by no fellowship or sympathy, but exercising more or less a spirit of persecution against each other, prevents an immensity of good that would arise, were the influence of the whole combined in objects of general usefulness. Without encroaching on the sacredness of religious belief there is a vast field for their associated exertions, in the support of schemes to instruct and improve mankind—to teach liberal and enlightened principles—to interest the feelings in the study or the contemplation of what is beautiful or useful in the wide domain of nature, or in the accumulated stores of science. The want of such combined power is shown in the wretched condition of society, not simply wretched from destitution, but from a pervading spirit of persecution that either openly disturbs the surface of social intercourse, or in an under current creates distrust, misrepresentations and ill feeling.

We have been led to make these remarks, which may, perhaps, appear foreign to the subject under consideration, from being familiar with the influence of such a spirit on the progress of the Philosophical Society, and of all similar institutions. So inveterate are prevailing prejudices, and so peculiarly sensitive are parties to the possibility of reflections on established truths, that the very term philosophy conjures up in imagination suspicions which elude definition, but are nevertheless real existences, and are productive of serious evils to the steady progress of truth, justice and charity.

The picture which is here presented has no exaggerated touches. It is an exact transcript from life, failing only

R 2

in the force of its delineations. Grateful indeed would be
the prospect, if we could see in the multiplication of
religious sects the dawning of a better spirit. We are
afraid, however, that this loses no portion of its bitterness
in its association with independent sentiments. It
is often much harsher in its manifestations, in every
successive degree of dissent, being accompanied with fewer
of the courtesies and refinements of polished life.

It is scarcely possible to imagine a more painful picture
than what is furnished by an analysis of the religious community. The diversity of sentiment and the severity which
accompanies the expression of it—each sect having the
consciousness of being right—and the indifference with
which each contemplates the eternal misery of all except
themselves, are some of the strange phenomena which fall
under our observation. The conviction, that millions will
inevitably be damned from an error in their creed, so far
from exciting a deep interest towards them in those who
are sure that *they* are in the just path, gives to the countenance an expression of complacency, and to the conduct
a peculiar softness of manner in ill accordance with
with the spirit which breathes from within. The worst
feature, however, in this state of things, is the neglected
condition of the great masses of the people. They are as
destitute of religion as if this were a part of dress to be put
on or taken off according to the fashion of the hour. In
their wretchedness, there is no temple that they visit in
search of consolation, and in their prosperity, none which
teaches by example the wisdom of moderation.

We are told that when christianity was first introduced,
the people had gradually declined in their attendance on

Pagan worship; and in the nineteenth century it is an unquestionable fact, that save the wealthy and the well dressed, the millions of a crowded population are grossly ignorant of the principles of christianity, and express no belief in them by any external forms. These are truths which ought not to be concealed in an inquiry into the condition of society; they are a part of the picture which it is our duty to sketch, and the most important, whether we consider present or future consequences. A tree bearing such fruit will, at no distant period, awaken attention, and in a manner that will afford abundant matter for reflection.

The members of the Philosophical Society are divided into two classes, proprietors and subscribers. The former pay annually two guineas—the latter one. The former are admitted to all public lectures and to the reading and discussion of all papers. The subscribers are allowed to attend the public lectures only. The committee are bound to furnish eight public lectures annually; the average number given is seldom, however, less than ten. In general men of distinguised literary or scientific attainments are engaged, so that in the course of a few years, a variety of interesting and useful subjects are brought under consideration. Papers are read monthly by the proprietors, and to these meetings a proprietor has the privilege of introducing two strangers resident in the town, under twenty-one years of age; and the subscriber has the same privilege in regard to the public lectures. The number of the proprietors is eighty-six, of which the manufacturers or merchants are only nineteen, the remainder being generally professional gentlemen or persons in easy circumstances following no particular pursuit. The subscribers are forty-eight, and of this number fourteen only are manufacturers or merchants. We state these facts, as evidence of the little literary or scientific interest associated with the progress of manufactures.

The Society possesses a museum exceedingly rich in geological and fossil specimens, as well as numerous curiosities in natural history, and the whole may be viewed every day from 11 to 4 o'clock, accompanied by a proprietor or subscriber, or having a note from either.

CHAPTER XXIII.

SCHOOL OF DESIGN.

Within the present month* a new institution, and one, calculated to be of great service, has come into existence, the object of which is to teach drawing, modelling and colouring. The following is the proposed plan :—

BRANCHES OF INSTRUCTION.

SECTION I.—ELEMENTARY INSTRUCTION.

I. DRAWING.

1. Outline Drawing.—Geometrical Drawing, Freehand Drawing.
2. Shadowing, the Use of Chalks, &c.
3. Drawing from Casts.
4. Drawing from Natural Objects, such as Fruit, Flowers, &c.

II. MODELLING.

From the Antique, &c.—From Nature.

III. COLOURING.

1. Instructions in the Use of Colours.—Water Colours; Oil Colours.

2. Colouring from Nature.

----

* July, 1843.

Section II.—Instructions as Applied to Industry.

Under this head, the necessary Instruction will be afforded, for applying the previous studies to the preparation of Designs, for the various branches of handicraft and manufacture, practised in Sheffield and its Vicinity, and for any other departments of industry to which the Committee from time to time may think the instructions of the School may be beneficially applied.

It is quite unnecessary to make any remarks to show the advantages of such a scheme, if liberally supported. Some of the important manufactures of the town, as the silver-plated, the white-metal, the stove-grate, and others, exercise to a large extent the inventive powers of the mind, as well as taste and skill in design; and the cultivation of these powers will be greatly facilitated by the occasions presented for systematic study. The undertaking is worthy of encouragement, not only from its direct application to the arts, but from its generally beneficial influence in elevating the views and improving the tone of the understanding. No one alive to the interests of the town can regard the formation of such an institution with indifference.

This is one of the first attempts of Government to meet the intellectual wants of the people, and we trust the results will show the wisdom of the step, and lead to the establishment of much more comprehensive measures in the same direction. The assistance which Government renders in the establishment of this school, is in the grant of £500, which is principally expended by them on models and in fitting up premises for effectually carrying out the objects contemplated. There is, also, an annual grant of £150, given on condition that the like sum is subscribed, which with considerable difficulty has been accomplished for the first year. One guinea subscription entitles the individual to nominate one student, who pays 8s. per quarter, if he attend the morning, and 4s. if he attend the evening school ; if not nominated by a subscriber, he pays 16s. and 8s. for the same instruction. The master is a person thoroughly familiar with the important duties which he has to perform.

Considering the nature of the advantages which are offered to the public,—the numerous and exquisitely finished plaister models and drawings, and the able tuition which is rendered, the charges are exceedingly moderate, and the advantages are such as money could not previously have purchased. The school is under the direction of a committee, among which are gentlemen of considerable taste and acquirements in the fine arts.

CHAPTER XXIV.

MEDICAL CHARITABLE INSTITUTIONS.

———

Among the noble institutions of the town conferring inestimable blessings on the poor, the Infirmary has the first claim upon our attention. From the year 1797, when it was opened, to the present time, it has been warmly supported by the public. The ample resources which it has at command, have been economized and expended with judgment, under the superintendence of men not less distinguished for intelligence than benevolence.* When we consider the broad principles of charity on which the institution is founded—that it is free to the necessitous of all nations, without distinction as to colour or creed ; and that within its doors are found kindness, attention and skill, according to the urgency of the case, it is unnecessary to expatiate on its usefulness. If of late years it has not received encouragement proportionate

———

* The present chairman is James Montgomery, Esq., of whose devotion to the interests of the institution it is impossible to speak in too high terms.

to the multiplied claims upon it, in justice to the public it ought to be stated, that benevolence is not limited now, as formerly, to one or two general objects, but is employed in ministering to the varied wants of suffering humanity, arising from the extension of manufactures and a greatly increased population. Within the past twenty years, numerous charities have sprung up, making additional demands upon the public, which will necessarily interfere with the degree of support rendered to previously established institutions.

In the following table are given several interesting particulars, for a series of years, connected with this institution :—

Particulars of the Out patients discharged annually from Midsummer 1822 *to Midsummer* 1838.

	Cured.	Relieved.	Own desire.	Non-attendance.	Not Relieved.	Incurable.	Made In patients.	Dead.
1823	971	488	35	230	89	3	35	38
1824	986	432	51	198	89	2	38	32
1825	983	452	25	234	60	4	31	25
1826	913	466	37	292	79	3	40	26
1827	1408	702	47	397	118	2	34	38
1828	1272	738	26	289	108	1	29	38
1829	1399	558	39	267	85	3	34	33
1830	1177	503	35	347	71	2	42	30
1831	1273	544	36	412	73	3	68	24
1832	1305	483	44	289	50	1	73	22
1833	1196	301	36	423	26	11	58	25
1834	909	241	31	260	35	5	50	28
1835	958	208	14	308	44	4	39	14
1836	961	195	22	282	38	9	53	28
1837	1059	229	22	434	30	7	75	16
1838	1282	265	31	464	27	5	65	25
1839	1230	239	11	356	16	2	71	44
1840	1396	241	39	400	34	8	55	32
1841	1717	320	36	369	0	5	50	22
	22395	7605	617	6251	1072	80	940	535

Particulars of the In-patients discharged annually, from Midsummer 1822 to Midsummer 1841.

	Cured.	Relieved.	For Irregularity.	Own desire.	Not Relieved.	Incurable.	Relieved. Made Out-patients.	Dead.
1823	293	68	6	8	7	0	316	16
1824	278	88	11	11	11	1	344	6
1825	305	109	7	28	12	0	326	15
1826	319	77	10	9	10	2	334	22
1827	417	121	9	18	9	2	407	31
1828	397	104	10	22	16	1	314	31
1829	408	87	9	14	12	0	291	31
1830	355	88	10	19	8	0	362	15
1831	315	79	14	17	15	1	363	12
1832	316	86	11	23	14	1	329	27
1833	336	42	38	16	8	4	394	22
1834	324	64	36	13	17	1	336	32
1835	363	59	35	18	8	2	329	28
1836	348	43	33	21	13	5	369	31
1837	364	60	38	28	11	4	421	77
1838	337	48	33	21	10	0	452	49
1839	317	64	20	15	6	6	431	65
1840	323	24	25	26	11	5	402	65
1841	366	34	30	32	9	6	354	36
	6481	1345	385	359	207	41	6874	611

As a medical officer attached to this institution for many years, we may, perhaps, be allowed to express an opinion on some points, which we conceive to be defects in the working of this, and, we are afraid, to some extent, of all similar charities. There is not sufficient discrimination exercised in the admission of patients. Numerous individuals become recipients of the advantages, who from the rate of their wages, small families or none at all, and other circumstances, have no legitimate right. The least part of the injury resulting is that which arises from the misdirection of the funds ;—a moral injury is inflicted of much greater importance to society. The respectable artisan is taught to depend on others in place of his own exertions, not only in a period of sickness, but in many other circumstances of life.   In a work which we published some years ago, on the abuses and evils of medical charities, these sentiments were expressed at some length, and evidence was adduced to show the justness of them.   The following is an extract from it :—

Of late years there has been a wide departure from the original intentions of the founders, and great violence done to the spirit of this charity, from want of clearly defined ideas in regard to the circumstances which entitle applicants to the benefits of it. When first established, it was for the poor and necessitous of all nations, and this of course was understood to mean, such only as were incapable of otherwise procuring the required aid.   It could not possibly have been contemplated that its blessings should be distributed indiscriminately to the working classes; that the fact of an individual being an operative furnished at once a sufficient claim.   We will not insult the memories of the good by a supposition so little in harmony with their enlightened benevolence.   Their consideration was for the poor and destitute, and not for the well-fed and well-paid operative.   He was not the object of their solicitude. Such, however, is the departure from the principles on which this institution was originally based, that it is now sufficient to be one of the working classes to be entitled to its benefit.   The artisan never dreams of the possibility of rejection on the ground of being in full and regular employment, and being amply remunerated for his labour.   He applies now as naturally to the charity when sick as he does to the tailor for the repair of his clothes, with this difference, that he would be perfectly astonished were any one to hint at the propriety of paying for the favours conferred by the former.   He regards the charity as his inherent right,—the unques. tionable right of labour, independent of any accompanying circumstances.   With this feeling of dependence and security, he has no motive to economise or to think for the future.

This is a state of things that ought not to be allowed to exist. If the door is to be thus thrown open it will cease to be an institution of charity, for this implies a ministering to necessities which would otherwise be neglected.   Specific laws are required to chalk out distinctly the objects worthy of relief.   It is not difficult to define some of the conditions which ought to exclude from a participation in the charity.

254 THE VITAL

In the first place, single men in employment have not the slightest claim. If they have failed to provide against the day of sickness when the opportunities were abundant, to relieve their wants is to teach them there is no necessity for careful and economical habits on their part. If they are not too ill to be incapacitated from pursuing their vocations, it is a gross imposition to extend to them the charity, and if otherwise, they have always homes. It may perhaps be urged in objection, that they will necessarily incur debts in providing at this time medical assistance. This, so far from being an objection, is an exceedingly powerful argument for throwing them upon their own resources. They will thus be taught practically the injurious effects of misconduct: the struggle to overcome the subsequent difficulties is indeed calculated to awaken reflection, and suggest rules for future guidance, than any discourse, however beautiful and just its views. The one leaves impressions which constantly intrude on the consideration of the mind; the other passes away with the dreams of morning.

Secondly. It could not possibly be contemplated to extend the charity to the married operative in work, with only a young and small family. What claim has he upon the funds of the Institution, certainly not those of destitution? Are his children to be taught from the moment they breathe, and is the lesson to be inculcated daily, to the years of maturity, that charity is the great good to which their aspirations are to be directed? Is indeed the first instruction to be that of dependence?

Thirdly. The operative receiving high wages, if he please to work, though he may have several children, can have no just claim on the charity. He has the means and he must be made to provide for the various wants of his family.

Fourthly. The operative who has several sons or apprentices working for him, is in no degree entitled to the benefits of the charity. His circumstances are very remote from those of destitution.

Fifthly. Neither male nor female servants in place, and attending to their respective duties, are proper objects of relief. To extend the charity to them is to save the pockets of their employers, which certainly was not contemplated in the formation of the institution. Those on whom we depend for comforts ought to be treated with much greater kindness and consideration. To direct their footsteps to a charity is, not to elevate, but to lower the moral sentiments.

The above conditions will perhaps be admitted, as amply sufficient to exclude improper objects from a participation in the benefits of a charitable institution; and some persons may probably be surprised to learn that, obvious and distinctive as they may appear in character, they have long ceased to invalidate the application of individuals. In evidence of this we shall shortly adduce indisputable facts. Before proceeding to this part of the inquiry, we shall bring under consideration circumstances which alone go far towards proving that charitable institutions are grossly imposed upon. The intelligent and reflecting mind will scarcely desire stronger evidence than these general facts. The distresses of a community will be admitted to bear a strict relation to the state of trade. When this is extremely depressed many hands are necessarily thrown out of employment. When it is good, the demand for labour is great, wages advance, and the blessings of plenty are universally experienced. The amount of misery or destitution cannot be the same in these very different circumstances. It cannot be a fixed quantity floating in society. The idea is absurd, and yet, if the registered demand for charity be any criterion of the misery existing, the quantity is scarcely subject to any variation whatever.

A few years ago it was found, that the Infirmary was inadequate to meet the demands of the poor, and laudable exertions were made to establish another institution, and the result was the present Dispensary. It has been liberally encouraged from the commencement, and some idea of the extent of its usefulness may be formed from the subjoined table, which states the number and the manner in which patients have been discharged:—

Years.	Cured.	Relieved.	Irregular or non-attendance.	Incurable.	Improper objects or improper conduct.	Infirmary.	Parish surgeon, or country.	Own desire.	Dead.	Total discharged and dead.	Remaining on the books.	Total.
1882*	1433	44	266	8	7*	5	3	2	76	1839	873	2712
1883	1789	118	194	7	6	5	8	2	77	2201	690	2891
1884	1529	80	160	7	4	2	2	8	59	1846	845	2691
1885	1864	158	561	8	1	6	8	6	105	2207	681	2888
1886	1266	101	207	9	4	12	3	16	110	1728	847	2575
1887	1738	141	172	29	6	17	14	13	84	2214	681	2895
1888	1643	116	402	6	6	28	16	8	95	2320	617	2937
1889	1779	110	460	4	9	32	•30	8	117	2549	496	3045
1840	1680	215	899	12	38	22	17	6	130	2519	418	2932

* The annual report gives these particulars from July of one year to July the next.

† Some few included in this column were discharged having been much longer on the books than the rules of the institution allow.

Many of the returns in this table, as in that connected
with the Infirmary, suggest a few remarks.   It will not for
a moment be imagined, that, in a period of manufacturing
prosperity, there is the same demand for gratuitous assistance, as in times of serious distress, and yet we perceive
that in the years 1834, 1835 and 1836, when trade was
in the most flourishing condition, the admissions were
much the same as in the three subsequent years, which
were times of severe and general depression.   It may
be urged, and with some truth, in answer to this objection, that the admissions are not an exact measure of
commercial suffering, depending on the number of subscribers or the amount subscribed.   Admitting the force of
this argument, it appears, however, that whatever may be
the means of relief, the demand is always equal to it.   We
will venture to assert that this will always be the case, not
simply because the means are inadequate to satisfy the
legitimate demands, but because the more expansive and
liberal the charity, and greater the inducements as well as
opportunities to take advantage of it.   We are not advocates
for the exercise of indiscriminate benevolence.   We would
aid the needy, but would not teach the well-paid artisan to
depend upon the exertions of others.

In the third column of the table, we observe the number
of individuals discharged for irregular or non-attendance.
From our knowledge of institutions of this kind we know,
that such are always understated.   The medical attendant
in looking over his book, finds that numerous parties have
not visited the charity for several weeks, and from his
recollection of the cases, or the description of the symptoms,
is certain that many of them must have been cured or at
least relieved, and they are accordingly so reported.   And

s

yet with all deductions, the number discharged in some years for non-attendance, is about one-fourth of the admissions. This is a large proportion of the applicants who have not had sufficient gratitude to thank the charity for gratuitious services conferred.

CHAPTER XXV.

LICENSED VICTUALLERS AND BEER HOUSE KEEPERS, IN THE PARISH OF SHEFFIELD.

TOWNSHIPS.	Licensed Victuallers.	BEER HOUSES.		Population in 1841.
		Liquor allwd to be drnk on the Premises	Not allowd to be drunk on the Premises	
Sheffield	292	371	81	69,587
Ecclesall Bierlow	51	80	15	19,984
Brightside Bierlow......	32	36	6	10,089
Attercliffe-cum-Darnall.	19	7	1	4,156
Hallam, Upper	7	8	1	1,401
Hallam, Nether	22	17	5	7,275
Totals......	423	519	109	112,492

It thus appears that in the township of Sheffield, containing a population of about 70,000, there are 292 inns and 371 beer-houses allowed to sell liquor on the premises; total, 663. This gives one to every 105 of the population. We are not acquainted with the ratios between such houses and the population in other towns, with the exception of Leeds. There the proportion is one to every 180 of the inhabitants. It is scarcely reasonable to imagine that houses of this decription would have increased to so great an extent, had not a demand for them been felt, hence, perhaps, the inference is inevitable, that the working classes here spend more of their weekly earnings in drink than the artisans in other manufacturing districts. This charge has often been urged, and it would appear from the foregoing facts

s 2

with some truth. The main causes of this dissipation, are the occasionally high wages received by the artisans, and the exhausting nature of the occupations. In some branches the labour is very severe, especially in many of the forging and grinding departments. The workmen in the cotton and woollen manufactures, in which machinery is largely employed, do not undergo any thing like the same amount of bodily labour.

One of the worst legislative measures ever enacted was the establishment of beer-houses, and they have done incalculable mischief ; they are often kept by persons destitute of capital and of questionable respectability ; consequently they are not very scrupulous or delicate about the character of their customers. The vicious and the abandoned of both sexes are received and encouraged by many of them ; and they have been the occasion of much crime, and a great increase of dissipation and immorality.

It was contemplated by Government, in the enactment of the measure respecting beer-houses, that the increase in the facilities for purchasing malt-liquor, not allowed to be drunk on the premises, would diminish the tendency to frequent such places. Had the designers of the bill been familiar with the habits and feelings of the working classes, they certainly would have formed no such anticipation.

CHAPTER XXVI.

THE TOWN-TRUST.

It was not our intention, in entering upon this inquiry, to make any remarks on the Corporate Institutions of the town. These have been described by a writer,* with a degree of accuracy equalled only by the beauty and simplicity of his style, and the fullness of mind that gives an interest to every object which he delineates ; and moreover as they undergo few modifications from the progress of time, further remarks would be superfluous. Had it been within the scope of our labours, to have brought under consideration distinguished individuals whom we claim as townsmen, whether dead or no longer resident among us, in neither class, and we hope he will long be numbered with the living, is there one name we should be prouder to record than that of Hunter. To him we are indebted for a vast portion of the interest which may be said to be inherent in numerous objects connected with the history of the town and neighbourhood, and which objects, without the animating influence of his pen, would soon have lost the kindling associations with which they are fraught. For the enduring life which his antiquarian skill has imparted to

* The History and Topography of the Parish of Sheffield, by the Rev. Joseph Hunter, F.A.S.

past times—to the localities in which we live, and for the
pleasure and instruction which his writings have afforded
us, we sincerely thank him.

Of all the Corporate or endowed institutions, the Town
Trust has, perhaps, undergone the greatest changes from
the increase of population and other circumstances. The
application of its funds has been modified at different
periods according to the extension or the necessities of the
town. At one time, they were employed in keeping in repair
a bridge; at another, in taking care of a pool of water, by
which the inhabitants, when few, were in part supplied; and
at a later date when the maintenance of the former fell
upon the riding, and the latter ceased to exist, they were
appropriated to the repair of the high ways, and subsequently to lighting the town. These objects being otherwise
provided for, the funds are now employed, and with great
discrimination, in improving the streets. Where the public
is inconvenienced from the narrowness of the road,
buildings are purchased and removed; and in the same
manner facilities of communication between different
parts of the town are promoted. In addition to this
annual application of a considerable sum, the Town Trust
is among the most liberal supporters of all important
charities, whether permanent or only temporary. We
cannot speak in too high terms of the openness and sound
judgment with which the affairs of the Trust have for
many years been managed. The accounts are published
annually, and every year exhibits local improvements,
which are to be traced to the judicious appropriation of the
funds.

Table shewing the Traffic on the Lady's Bridge and the Iron Bridge.

Saturday, Dec. 11, 1841.	LADY'S BRIDGE.				IRON BRIDGE.
Hour.	Carriages of every description.	Foot-passengers, N.W. side.	Foot-passengers S.E. side.	Total foot-passengers.	Foot-passengers.
A.M. 7 to 8	64	337	202	539	441
... 8 to 9	101	528	287	815	644
... 9 to 10	162	537	360	897	536
... 10 to 11	189	648	383	1031	458
... 11 to 12	125	697	431	1128	521
P.M. 12 to 1	132	1006	496	1502	1257
... 1 to 2	136	766	411	1177	880
... 2 to 3	187	713	391	1104	527
... 3 to 4	199	826	536	1362	432
... 4 to 5	212	846	557	1403	1101
... 5 to 6	104	901	536	1437	855
... 6 to 7	81	798	689	1487	797
... 7 to 8	60	1167	691	1858	817
... 8 to 9	65	1012	643	1655	902
... 9 to 10	46	759	510	1269	777
Total ...	1,863	11,541	7,123	18,664	10,945
Monday, Dec. 13, 1841.					
A.M 7 to 8	53	289	156	445	437
... 8 to 9	130	664	415	1079	849
... 9 to 10	207	858	417	1275	902
.. 10 to 11	176	886	533	1419	1007
... 11 to 12	171	831	484	1315	590
P.M. 12 to 1	134	1263	615	1878	1293
... 1 to 2	126	967	506	1473	950
... 2 to 3	150	795	372	1167	601
... 3 to 4	169	797	417	1214	567
... 4 to 5	154	869	421	1281	1050
... 5 to 6	124	741	437	1178	745
... 6 to 7	82	801	523	1324	720
... 7 to 8	56	895	533	1428	1121
... 8 to 9	60	838	464	1302	801
... 9 to 10	25	465	354	819	706
Total	1,817	11,950	6,647	18,597	12,339
Grand total 2 days ...	3,680	23,491	13,770	37,261	23,284

SHEFFIELD :
J. H. GREAVES, PRINTER, COMMERCIAL BUILDINGS.

CPSIA information can be obtained at www.ICGtesting.com
Printed in the USA
BVOW01s1142071113

335713BV00014B/214/P